AF263689

History of Scotland

Discovering Lost Stories from Scottish History

Free Bonus from Captivating History (Available for a Limited time)

Hi History Lovers!

Now you have a chance to join our exclusive history list so you can get your first history ebook for free as well as discounts and a potential to get more history books for free!

Simply visit the link below to join.

Or, Scan the QR code!

captivatinghistory.com/ebook

Also, make sure to follow us on Facebook, X, and YouTube by searching for Captivating History.

Table of Contents

Introduction

Today, Scotland is known for many things. Some cannot help but imagine its serene, yet mysterious Highlands, often cloaked in mists. Others are intrigued by the deep lochs, a few of which are said to be the dwellings of magical creatures. A few may recall the Scottish accent, which is typically remembered for its strong rolling "r" and a rhythmic, almost sing-song quality that sets it apart from other accents. But, of course, beneath these familiar images lies a collection of stories that reaches back centuries, if not millennia.

Long before people called it "Scotland," the land was home to scattered tribes. They shared the land, but there were many instances when they invaded each other, formed alliances, and then betrayed each other. Scotland was once a wild northern frontier of the Roman Empire. The people of the land witnessed the Roman legions pouring into their homeland and tasted their disciplined wrath, yet the Romans never succeeded in fully conquering them. The fierce tribes always retaliated with fury to the point where the Romans decided to build walls to keep them at bay.

When Rome eventually saw its influence wane, its retreat from the region left a power vacuum, resulting in the rise of competing kingdoms. In the southwest was the Kingdom of Strathclyde, ruled by Britons who had once lived under Roman influence but now forged their own path. To the west, across the sea, came settlers from Ireland (the Gaelic-speaking Scots) who established the Kingdom of Dál Riata in Argyll and the Hebrides. These early Scots brought not just a language (Gaelic) but also a new royal bloodline and a deep sense of spiritual mission.

Of course, we cannot forget the Picts. They lived on the lands farther east and south (including areas like Fife, Angus, Aberdeenshire, and Moray). Their language has all but vanished, and their stories are incomplete, yet it is safe to assume that the Picts were central to Scotland's early identity. In the southeast were the Gododdin, descendants of the ancient Britons whose warriors were immortalized in heroic poetry. All of these kingdoms were often at war with one another, but they shared blood, beliefs, and shifting alliances that would eventually create the foundations of a unified realm.

In the 9th century, the land experienced the beginning of a change. The Pictish and Gaelic kingdoms, under mounting pressure from Norse invasions, began to join arms. The man often credited with uniting them was Kenneth MacAlpin, a king of Dál Riata who, through conquest, diplomacy, or perhaps even marriage, succeeded in bringing the Picts under his rule. Thus, the Kingdom of Alba was born; it was known to be the earliest recognizable form of what would become Scotland. Alba stretched from the River Forth to the Highlands and beyond.

Unity, however, never promised peace. New challenges soon arose. As Alba's kings extended their influence southward, they came into increasing contact—and conflict—with the emerging power of England. The English kings, especially under the Norman and Plantagenet dynasties, would express their refusal to accept Scotland as an equal. Instead, the English viewed the kingdom as a land ripe for vassalage, if not outright conquest. Battles and rebellions became a regular occurrence, and treaties were as common as betrayals.

Still, the Scots were undeterred; they resisted fiercely despite constantly finding themselves outnumbered or outmatched. Out of this long struggle, the world saw the emergence of figures who remain icons of Scottish national identity, from warrior kings to rebel lords, knights, and ladies who stood defiant despite having to face relentless siege or perhaps death itself.

Chapter 1 – Clans and Their Feuds

Some say in the Highlands, blood runs thicker than water and longer than memory. To belong to a clan was to carry the weight of ancestry and the burden of honor. Your surname would not only identify you; it could also open doors for unimaginable opportunities or ignite feuds. A clan could be a political force, a military unit, and even a code of conduct passed from one generation to the next. In a kingdom where central governance was, more often than not, distant and unreliable, it was your chief, siblings, cousins, and tartan that gave you protection and purpose.

In the eyes of outsiders, these clans could be seen as old-fashioned or chaotic family groups from the distant past. But for the Scots, especially those in the Highlands and Western Isles (the Outer Hebrides), the clan system was the framework of their lives. It shaped everything from marriage and law to songs and legends. Some clans rose to prominence through alliances with kings. Others had to walk more challenging paths where they faced being outlawed, hunted, or, even worse, erased from history.

Clan MacGregor, the Name None Dared To Bear

To the untrained eye, the morning seemed calm at first. Mist rolled low over Glen Fruin (a narrow valley near Loch Lomond) just as the sun was about to rise between the rolling hills. Then, suddenly, the peaceful sight was replaced with a sense of unease. Nearly four hundred foot soldiers, complete with mail shirts and armed with hagbuts, pistols, axes, and two-handed swords, marched to the glen. They were from the MacGregor clan. On the other side of the battlefield was a bigger force from the Colquhoun clan, which boasted both infantry units and mounted soldiers.

The Colquhouns were a powerful Lowland clan. They had long called the lands around Loch Lomond their home. With their chief stronghold located at Luss, which lay on important routes between the Highlands and Lowlands, the clan had massive control over the surrounding fertile lands and trade routes. The Colquhouns had also built a firm trust with the Crown. They were often seen as upholders of royal authority, especially in contrast to clans like the MacGregors, who frequently found themselves in conflict with the law. This connection likely gave the Colquhouns better access to arms, horses, and support, making them, on paper at least, better equipped and prepared for open battle.

Clan MacGregor claimed to have been descended from the old kings of Dalriada. Therefore, they were of royal blood. They lived in the steep glens of Perthshire. These lands, however, were seldom merciful. Surviving here required resilience; perhaps this was why the MacGregors grew to be so fierce and independent. The rugged, mountainous terrain of Glen Strae, Glen Orchy, and Glen Lyon, as well as the cold and wet climate, made it difficult for the people to cultivate the land. The clan relied heavily on cattle herding as a result. Cattle were a form of wealth to these people. They were used not only for trade but also for dowries and even rent. The MacGregors, like many other Highland clans, would go on cattle raids, especially in times of scarcity and conflict. They raided neighboring clans, particularly those in the Lowlands.

In the late 1500s, the MacGregors got into trouble with their neighbors. The clan was accused of committing two crimes against the Colquhouns, who were under the leadership of Sir Alexander Colquhoun. The MacGregor clan was said to have stolen cattle from the Colquhouns and killed two of their men. Coupled with their already existing tension, the Colquhouns chose to show their wrath. Upon receiving the blessing of King James VI to suppress the MacGregors by force, the Colquhouns immediately made their move. An army of around seven hundred men, largely composed of cavalry, was sent to confront the MacGregors at Glen Fruin.

The fierce MacGregors were always ready for battle. Led by Allaster MacGregor of Glenstrae, the MacGregor forces were split into two divisions. They knew that the battlefield was not suitable for mounted forces, so an ambush was set in the hopes they could make use of the terrain to trap their enemy in the narrow part of the glen.

Their plans worked. The Colquhoun cavalry found it extremely difficult to maneuver on the boggy ground. They eventually found themselves surrounded by their enemy. Without hesitation, the MacGregors charged and struck their enemies. Many of the cavalry lost their balance to hold their ground. They slipped and fell into the deep, treacherous moss near the farm of Auchengaich. Some of the Colquhoun men broke ranks while others were cut down where they stood. The defeat was devastating. Nearly two hundred Colquhouns died in battle, while the MacGregors only lost two lives, though some sources debate the accuracy of that.

Even though the MacGregors emerged victorious, what happened next stained the name of their clan for generations. Rumors swirled across the land, painting the MacGregors as ruthless barbarians. They were said to have spared no one. Not only did they butcher the soldiers, but the MacGregors also killed women and children. This claim was never proven, but people at that time believed it.

King James VI, who was intent on breaking Highland resistance, wasted no time in taking action against the clan. He outlawed the MacGregor name in 1603. Allaster MacGregor was executed in 1604, along with eleven of his chieftains. The Crown made it legal to hunt anyone who bore the name MacGregor. The Battle of Glen Fruin had led to a collective punishment.

Yet, the MacGregors were never fully erased despite the Crown's efforts. Some lived under false surnames like Murray, Grant, and Black. Others continued to live the life of an outlaw, calling the forests and mountains their homes. The clan remained proscribed for well over a century. It was only in 1774 that the name MacGregor was legally restored by an act of Parliament. Full recognition of the clan happened in 1822 when King George IV sat on the throne.

Clan Macfie and the Capture of Its Last Chief

Malcolm Macfie could be seen standing atop a rocky rise, overlooking the sea. His face was tight as he observed the many boats approaching the shores of Colonsay. The island, located in the Inner

Hebrides, was the home of Clan Macfie. This Gaelic-speaking clan traced their lineage to Dubside, one of the legendary Siol Alpin, the ancient kin group believed to descend from Alpin, father of Kenneth MacAlpin, first king of the Scots. Ever since the 13th century, the Macfies held influence over Colonsay and parts of Oronsay.

Their size was rather modest when compared to the mainland clans, but the Macfies commanded respect in the Hebrides. However, despite their authority over neighboring islanders, the Macfies were also constantly entangled in the turbulent politics of Scotland.

The clan had always served the Lord of the Isles, a position that was held by MacDonald chieftains. When the lordship fell to the Scottish Crown in the late 15th century, it disrupted the islanders' centuries-old networks of allegiance and protection. Clans like the Macfies, who had once thrived under the semi-autonomous MacDonald rule, now found themselves isolated and exposed in a rapidly centralizing kingdom where loyalty to the Crown often came second to past associations.

Malcolm Macfie was the last chieftain to rule Colonsay under the clan's independent name. His loyalty, however, was complex, especially since there were times when the Macfies' relationship with the MacDonalds soured due to local disputes and competition for influence in the Inner Hebrides. Yet, despite the fights, the Macfies sided with Sir James MacDonald when he chose to rebel against the Scottish Crown and its ally, Clan Campbell, particularly the earls of Argyll.

The rebellion was sparked when the Scottish Crown granted lands that traditionally belonged to the MacDonalds to the Campbells and another clan known as the MacLeans. This was viewed as an encroachment by Sir James. Tensions simmered, eventually boiling over in 1598. Sir James fought against the MacLean clan at the Battle of Traigh Ghruinneart, killing the clan's chief, Sir Lachlan MacLean.

Malcolm Macfie allied with Sir James throughout the entire course of the rebellion. But the rebellion was not meant to last. To escape royal retribution, Sir James fled to Ireland. Those who once aligned with the fleeing chief were marked as the next targets by the Crown.

This was the moment the Campbells were waiting for. Led by Coll MacDonald of Colkitto, the cousin of Sir James, who aligned with the Campbells, a force was amassed to obliterate the Macfies. The exact details are murky, but Malcolm Macfie and eighteen others were captured and handed to the earl of Argyll. However, they were given a deal. Their lives would be spared under the condition that they serve on the government's side and fight against the remaining rebels.

Malcolm chose his life. For a time, he remained on Colonsay along with Coll MacDonald. However, peace was never an option between the two. Again, the details are uncertain, but Malcolm found himself on the run across the land he once called home. Legend has it that Malcolm tried to hide from his pursuers until a gull that was circling overhead betrayed his position. He was eventually captured by Coll MacDonald's men and tied to a rock before being shot.

With Malcolm's death, the Macfies lost their ancestral stronghold. Although Coll MacDonald had fought under a banner aligned with Clan Campbell, Colonsay did not fall into their hands. Instead, Coll MacDonald took the island for himself and held control over it for several years until it was eventually absorbed into the earldom of Argyll.

Of course, this was not the last time we heard about Clan Macfie. In the late 20th century, a global movement among Macfie descendants sought to restore their heritage. Thanks to the efforts of historians and genealogists, Clan Macfie was officially recognized by the Court of the Lord Lyon (a court of law that oversees heraldry) in 1981, and a modern chief was elected.

The Wrath of MacNab

A messenger rode hard along the banks of Loch Tay. He was racing to deliver grim news to the MacNab chief. The clan's servant had gotten in trouble. He had been tasked by the MacNab chief on Christmas to travel to the town of Crieff and gather provisions for the upcoming festivities. However, on his way back, the servant was stopped and beaten. The provisions that he had collected were robbed. The unfortunate news enraged the MacNab chief. The clan had made many enemies throughout the years, but they knew exactly who was behind the attack: Clan Neish.

For generations, the MacNabs had claimed descent from Abraruadh, a figure believed to have been the abbot of Glen Dochart and Strathearn. Even their Gaelic name, Mac an Aba, meant "the son of the abbot." The MacNabs saw their influence spread across lands that lay around Killin and the shores of Loch Tay. Interestingly, for much of their early history, the MacNabs were overshadowed by larger neighbors like the Campbells of Breadalbane, the Drummonds, and the Menzies. But still, the clan endured for many years, sometimes through marriage and other times through violence.

One of their greatest enemies was the Neish clan. Despite being humble in size, this clan was as fierce as it was stubborn. Its members often raided MacNab lands and refused to submit. Their feuds went on for years, and their confrontations often involved ambushes and petty thefts. This tale involving the robbery of their servant was the final straw. The MacNabs were eager to put an end to Clan Neish.

And so, the MacNab chief laid out his plan. He picked twelve men, those whom he believed were the strongest and most trustworthy. This included a man named Iain Mion Mac Appa, or Smooth John MacNab. He was popular among the people for being strong and athletic. When it was time to launch their revenge attack, these men hoisted a longboat onto their shoulders and made their way to Loch Earn. When they arrived, the men continued their journey by quietly rowing their boats to Neish Island.

The story goes that the MacNabs arrived just before dawn. Still benefiting from the cover of darkness, they carefully drew their weapons and wreaked havoc on their enemies using the element of surprise. Every Neish man was brutally slain that night, save for only two who managed to hide underneath their beds. Not content with the massacre, the MacNabs plundered and took as much as they could carry. Before leaving, they severed the heads of the fallen ones and carried them back to Killin. The severed heads were presented before the MacNab chief as proof that they had accomplished their revenge mission.

By the 17th and 18th centuries, the MacNabs, like other clans, were caught up in the turbulence of Scottish politics. Although traditionally a Highland clan, their loyalties in the Jacobite uprisings of the early 18th century were divided. The Jacobites were supporters of the exiled Stuart royal family, who sought to restore James VII of Scotland (James II of England) and his descendants to the British throne after they were displaced by the Glorious Revolution. The clan chief, John MacNab, supported the Hanoverian government and served in the Black Watch regiment. He was captured after the Battle of Prestonpans in 1745. However, many other MacNabs sided with Prince Charles Edward Stuart and fought with the Jacobites.

After the Battle of Culloden, Clan MacNab, like many Highland clans, faced the harsh repercussions of the British government's crackdown. Under the Disarming Act and subsequent Acts of Proscription, the clan was required to surrender its weapons. Traditional clan authority was dismantled, and the chiefs were stripped of their ancient status. The government also banned the wearing of tartan and Highland dress, striking at the heart of Gaelic cultural identity.

By the mid-18th century, the MacNabs were already under financial strain. The aftermath of Culloden only deepened their decline, as debts mounted and clan lands were gradually sold to repay creditors. Yet, even as their power faded in Scotland, the MacNab name would find new life overseas.

In the early 19th century, Archibald MacNab, the seventeenth chief, emigrated to Canada following bankruptcy. There, he established MacNab Township in Ontario and styled himself "the Laird of MacNab," bringing with him the pride of his lineage. His life was marked by both ambition and controversy, but he remained a MacNab through and through, preserving the spirit of the clan across the Atlantic.

The Betrayal That Caught the Gunns by Surprise

Everyone went silent when a stranger walked by, bearing scars across his face and arms, the kind that were caused by blades and axes. Some offered him bread, but only a few dared to ask him questions. He later left, but his story lingered, becoming the talk of the town. The man belonged to Clan Gunn. He was also one of the few survivors of a massacre that took place in 1478.

The Gunns were a Norse Gaelic clan from Caithness and Sutherland. They claimed descent from Gunni, one of the grandsons of the Viking Sweyn Asleifsson, who famously went on a rampage in the 12th century. When Norse influence finally waned in Scotland's north, the Gunns began to adapt Gaelic customs. But they still retained their fierce nature and independence. The Gunns were also considered among the earliest clans to emerge in the far-flung northern Highlands, far from the politics of the Lowlands or royal courts. Known for their martial prowess, many from the clan served as sheriffs or judges in Caithness. This made them both respected and resented.

The clan's greatest enemy was Clan Keith. Their rivalry was said to have begun in the late 15th century. Their feud soon spiraled from mere skirmishes into violent bloodshed. One of the most infamous chapters of their long and bitter rivalry was the Battle of Champions, fought in 1478 or 1464. This trial by combat was meant to end the decades-long hostilities between the two clans, though it only deepened the wound.

It was rare for the two clans to reach an agreement, so when both finally agreed to hang up their weapons after the trial, some were hopeful that peace would soon follow. The location was then set. Both clans were to pick twelve men to participate in an honorable duel at the Chapel of St. Tears near Ackergill. The rules were simple. Twelve men would go up against twelve rivals, with swords only and no treachery. The Gunns adhered to the rules, but the Keiths had something else in mind. Unknown to the Gunns, they brought twenty-four men. These additional twelve hid until the fight began.

What followed was a massacre. The outnumbered Gunns were ambushed. Still, they fought with ferocity. Unfortunately, many fell to the swords of the betraying Keiths. Their rivalry continued for centuries. Retaliation became more common than ever, with each act more brutal than the last.

Suffice it to say that the feud between the two clans left a deep stain on northern Scotland. Families were split, alliances shifted, and the Highlands grew bloodier. The memory of the chapel ambush became part of clan lore, a cautionary tale passed down around hearths and in hushed tones after the sun set.

The Gunns continued to wear their tartan with pride and guarded their heritage and culture. Over time, the clan dispersed. Some moved to the Lowlands, while others emigrated, particularly to Canada and New Zealand. The chiefship lay dormant for centuries after 1785, but in 1978, clan members resolved to restore it. A peace treaty was signed that year with Clan Keith, ending their historic feud. After decades of effort, Iain Alexander Gunn of Banniskirk was formally recognized in 2015 by the Lord Lyon King of Arms as chief of Clan Gunn, the first such chief in about 230 years. He died in 2024, and his son, John, took on the role.

The Clan Chattan Confederation

Two groups of warriors, each with thirty men, could be seen facing one another. It was the year 1396, and they met on the green stretch of the North Inch of Perth. These warriors were not alone. A short distance away was a wooden grandstand that had been erected a few days before. It was reserved for King Robert III and his court, who were sitting, ready to watch the spectacle unfold. This was not an ordinary battle between clans. It was a trial by combat, and it was to end a bitter blood feud between the members of Clan Chattan and Clan Cameron.

In contrast to other Highland clans, which were typically bound by blood, the Clan Chattan was a confederation. It was a union of allied families who chose to join arms for mutual protection and strength. At the center of this confederation were the Mackintoshes. The rest included the Macphersons, Davidsons, MacGillivrays, MacBeans, and several others. Together, they held sway over large parts of Badenoch and Inverness-shire.

The origins of the confederation are rather murky. Some spoke of stories of a marriage union between the Macphersons and the Mackintoshes, while others claimed their alliance was born out of necessity during the Wars of Scottish Independence, a time when chaos and violence spread across the kingdom, leading scattered families to band together under a common cause. Whatever its origins, the confederation endured, operating as a kind of Highland federation in which each clan retained its own identity while swearing loyalty to the central leadership.

When the world entered the closing of the 14th century, Clan Chattan found itself locked in a violent feud with its long-standing enemy, Clan Cameron. The reasons behind their animosity were similar to many other Highland disputes. They fought over territory, cattle raids, and other slights that had compounded over generations. For many years, blood was spilled across the hills of Lochaber and Badenoch, yet there were no signs of the clans putting an end to their hostilities. And so, it was high time for the Crown to step in. Weary of the endless bloodshed that had disrupted royal authority and trade, the king demanded a resolution. A plan was laid that demanded the two clans select thirty champions to fight in Perth under the king's and his court's supervision. They would let battle decide who held the rightful claim.

Perhaps eager to end the violence once and for all, the clans agreed. While it is widely decided that the trial by combat was a contest between Clan Chattan and Clan Cameron, interestingly, there are suggestions that the Camerons were not even involved. This suggests that it was the Macphersons and Davidsons within Clan Chattan who fought amongst themselves over primacy. Still, whatever the truth, the violence that followed was indescribable.

We can imagine fierce scenes of axes clashing against broadswords and of the green field slick with blood in just minutes. Then, one man, realizing his side was doomed, leaped into the River Tay. Though it seemed like death was only a step closer to reaching him, the man managed to escape by swimming. His name is unknown, but his act was recorded. When the slaughter finally ended, only eleven men remained standing.

Clan Chattan emerged victorious that day, but it was a bitter kind of glory. The field of the North Inch bore the scars of their ferocity. The king might have been entertained, but the Highlands knew the cost. Feuds might pause, but they rarely vanish completely.

Over the centuries, the confederation's clans rose and fell in influence. The Mackintoshes, as captains of Clan Chattan, wielded considerable power and often found themselves entangled in Highland politics. In the Jacobite risings of 1715 and 1745, various branches of the confederation took different sides. Some chose to fight for the Stuarts, while others fought for the Hanoverians. So, the unity of the confederation endured, but internal tensions were always close to the surface.

Chapter 2 – Men Born for Battle

William Wallace might have been familiar to many, especially those who have watched the 1990s movie *Braveheart*. The scene of Wallace's death left a mark on the modern audience. When the camera closes in on Wallace's face, he seems to be in terrible pain. Bound in a cruciform position on a wooden platform before an English crowd, he faces torture—possibly disembowelment, although the camera never pans to his lower torso—while a priest whispers into his ear, urging him to plead for a merciful death. Yet, despite the pain, the Scottish hero refuses to do so. Instead, he gathers all the voice he has left and shouts, "Freedom!"

His focus then shifts to the crowds, where a vision of his deceased wife suddenly appears, smiling at him. Meanwhile, the masked executioner steps forward and drops the ax, beheading Wallace. William Wallace, the hero of the people, dies a martyr's death. The scene stirs hearts. Yet, as powerful as that scene is, it spares the audience from the full horror of Wallace's real death.

A statue of William Wallace at Aberdeen.[1]

In reality, William Wallace faced one of the cruelest methods of execution in the medieval period. It was carried out as a public display of political vengeance. The English Crown did not want to simply eradicate him, let alone make him a martyr. They wished to make him an example, to terrify those who planned on defying the Crown.

William Wallace was born around 1270. In contrast to Hollywood's depiction of him, Wallace was far from a poor peasant who spent his days toiling the land. He was born into a minor noble family in Elderslie, Renfrewshire. Though not of great wealth, Wallace was given a chance to receive a knight's training. He was taught the art of swordplay, horsemanship, and possibly even Latin. It is safe to conclude that he was literate, multilingual, and very much a man of status, if not of the court.

He first walked the path of rebellion when Scotland entered a period of despair. King Alexander III had unexpectedly died in 1286. Since his children had all died before him, there was no heir to the throne. Scotland was immediately plunged into succession chaos. This was viewed as a golden opportunity by Edward I of England. Also known as Edward Longshanks or the Hammer of the Scots, the king intervened under the guise of arbitration. He installed John Balliol as the next king of the Scots, only to strip him of his royal status when Balliol refused to follow his commands and signed a treaty with France.

With Balliol out of the picture, Edward I began asserting his power over Scotland. He seized the Stone of Destiny, which was used for centuries in the coronation of Scottish kings. He kept it beneath the English throne in Westminster Abbey. Without a king and a functioning government, Scotland fell under military occupation. English soldiers occupied castles, enforced taxes, and demanded loyalty. Many Scottish nobles, fearing for their lives, swore fealty to Edward. Others, however, refused to bow down to a foreigner. William Wallace was one of those who never hesitated to rise in defiance.

In 1297, he led an ambush against the English officials at Lanark. Some said he was driven by vengeance; his wife, Marion Braidfute, had been murdered by the sheriff of Lanark. Others claim this was nothing more than a legend since her name only appeared in written records two centuries following Wallace's death. Regardless of the existence of Marion, we can be sure that Wallace's rebellion escalated rather quickly. On September 11th, 1297, Wallace and another resistance leader, Andrew Moray, faced a larger English force at the famous Battle of Stirling Bridge. Victory belonged to the Scots, though Moray died weeks later from the wounds he obtained on the battlefield. Wallace was knighted and named the Guardian of Scotland.

Of course, this was not the last time we saw William Wallace on the battlefield. The following year, he led his troops against Edward's full might at the Battle of Falkirk. However, this time around, the English forces gained the upper hand. Wallace was left with no choice but to retreat. He resigned the guardianship and chose to move quietly, engaging only in guerrilla warfare. For years, he succeeded in evading capture. Sources claimed he traveled far, reaching France and even Rome to seek support. Still, his fate had already been written.

His fall began with a betrayal. He was eventually captured near Glasgow in 1305 when a Scottish knight named John Menteith sold information about Wallace's whereabouts and his next moves to Edward I. The reason behind his treachery varies. While some said he did so to receive the sheriffdom of Dumbarton as a reward, others lean toward personal vendetta; his nephew was killed in the Battle of Falkirk. Another version of the betrayal points to Wallace's own servant, Jack Short. He was said to have betrayed Wallace to settle a vendetta as well. His brother had been slain by Wallace, and he could also claim the bounty offered by Edward I.

William Wallace was transported to London in chains, and on August 23rd, 1305, he was brought to Westminster Hall. Of course, the trial was nothing more than just a performance. The Englishmen had already made up their minds before Wallace even set foot in London. He was neither permitted to speak in his own defense nor given counsel.

As expected, Wallace was found guilty in a trial that offered no real chance of defense. He was charged with treason, murder, and rebellion. Historical sources record that Wallace firmly rejected the treason charge, arguing that he had never sworn allegiance to Edward I and therefore could not be a traitor. This defense made no difference to the court. For treason, he was sentenced to the full punishment. He would be drawn through the streets, hanged until near death, disemboweled, castrated, beheaded, and quartered.

The English did not waste their time carrying out the brutal punishment. On the same day, they stripped Wallace naked and tied him to a wooden hurdle (similar to a makeshift sled). He was then dragged by horses from the Tower of London to Smithfield. The street stretched nearly six miles long. The punishment was held in public; crowds quickly lined the streets to witness the humiliation of the headstrong rebel—or hero in the eyes of the Scots. Some threw rotten food, stones, feces, and garbage as he passed. There were also those who struck him with rods as they spat curses in his face.

This was only the beginning of the horror. At Smithfield in London, William Wallace was hanged by the neck, left dangling until he was nearly unconscious. This was not meant to kill him, only to weaken him before further punishment. He was then cut down. While still alive, Wallace was castrated, his genitals severed and likely burned afterward, as was customary in executions for high treason. Next, his abdomen was opened, and his intestines were slowly pulled out and burned, a procedure meant to prolong his suffering and humiliate him. Some accounts claim the crowd could smell the burning flesh. Later stories also suggest Wallace was still alive when his heart was removed, but no contemporary chronicle confirms this. Only after this series of tortures was he beheaded. His body was then quartered, with his limbs sent to Newcastle, Berwick, Stirling, and Perth as a warning to others. His head, tarred for preservation, was displayed on a pike atop London Bridge.

A plaque marking the place of Wallace's execution.[2]

These extremely brutal punishments were meant to crush the Scottish resistance, but they failed. Scotland's fight continued under Robert the Bruce, and just nine years later, the Scots won a decisive victory at the Battle of Bannockburn in 1314. It wasn't until 1328, however, that England formally recognized Scotland's independence.

The First Recorded Scot to Resist Invasion

William Wallace was not the first to have had his body torn apart in the name of resistance. Nor was he the first to defy foreign rule. Many centuries before Scotland even got its name, long before kings and knights scoured the land, another warrior stood his ground, defending the land he was so familiar with against an invading power. His name, at least the one we've been given, was Calgacus.

A depiction of Calgacus giving his speech to the Caledonians.*

Interestingly, he was mentioned in only a single source, and even then, it was secondhand. Calgacus's name was included in the biography of the Roman general Gnaeus Julius Agricola. It was written sometime in 98 CE by the general's son-in-law, the Roman historian Tacitus.

According to ancient sources, the Romans had conquered much of southern Britannia by the early 80s CE. Fortified towns were constructed, Roman law was introduced to the local populations, and temples dedicated to the Roman gods started to dot the region. However, northern Britain, the very land where Scotland lies, proved far more difficult for the Romans to assert their control.

The Romans referred to the region as Caledonia and its people as Caledonians. The Caledonians were not a united people. Many tribal societies called northern Britannia home. They had no written language and often fought among themselves, but even the Romans agreed they were not an easy foe. Despite their military lacking the discipline of the Roman legions, their warriors were fierce, and all of them had a deep knowledge of the land.

General Agricola launched a campaign to pacify the north in 77 CE. Not only did the Romans build roads and start constructing forts as far north as Inverness, but they also burned settlements, laid waste to farmlands, and captured hostages. But still, the Caledonians refused to give up their freedom and bow down to the invading Romans. Skirmishes and bloodshed became a common occurrence.

Then, about a decade after the start of the campaign, either in 83 or 84 CE, the Roman army faced a unified force of Caledonian warriors. Tacitus recorded that at least thirty thousand Caledonian warriors gathered somewhere in the Grampian Mountains, ready to face the Roman army. At the forefront of the line was the chieftain Calgacus.

Tacitus's writings about Calgacus were brief; he did not provide a description of the warrior or talk about his background. He did, however, recall Calgacus's thunderous speech that condemned the Roman Empire: "They ravage, they slaughter, they seize by false pretenses, and all of this they call empire; and where they make a desert, they call it peace."[i]

No one can verify whether those words actually came from Calgacus. Many scholars argue about whether Calgacus even existed in the first place; he could have been nothing more than a literary invention by Tacitus, designed to criticize Rome's greed. Others believe differently. Tacitus might have Latinized Calgacus's name. There are also theories

---

[i] Tacitus. *The Germany and the Agricola of Tacitus.*
https://www.gutenberg.org/files/7524/7524-h/7524-h.htm

that Calgacus was a title; some suggest his name was related to the Gaelic word *calgach*, which is translated as "fierce." If that was the case, Tacitus might have misunderstood his name.

The two armies clashed with each other at dawn, possibly near the modern-day Bennachie or Knock Hill in Aberdeenshire. While the Romans had an army of twenty thousand men, the Caledonians had mustered about thirty thousand warriors, though this number may be inflated. The battle opened with an exchange of missiles between the two armies. The Caledonian chariots then charged down the slope in waves. Their weapons were simple compared to those of the Romans. They were armed with swords, spears, and shields made from hide and wood. Some wore helmets, but many did not.

Still, they were absolutely fierce and had the high ground. Only their front ranks were on the level ground. Others were stationed up the slope of the hill in a horseshoe formation. One thing they lacked was the Roman army's discipline. When Agricola ordered the advancement of the Roman auxiliaries, the Caledonians were pushed back up the hill.

Undeterred, the Caledonians up the hill attempted a flanking maneuver. However, the Romans got to them first, and they were outflanked by the Roman cavalry. It is safe to say that the terrain that had favored them in many battles and skirmishes before now worked against them. Many fell that day. Tacitus claimed the Caledonians lost 10,000 lives, while the Romans only lost 360 auxiliary troops. The surviving Caledonians retreated into the woods. The Romans pursued them the next morning to no avail. It is said that the Caledonians were never to be found; they seemed to have disappeared into thin air. There were also no records of Calgacus being killed or captured. Perhaps he was among those who fell on the battlefield, or perhaps he lived and continued to resist the imperial forces in the years that followed, eventually fading into the landscape like so many warriors whose names were never written down.

As for Rome, the empire claimed victory that day, but its control over the Caledonians did not last. The Caledonians continued to resist. Eventually, the Romans were left with no choice but to retreat south. They built Hadrian's Wall and, two decades later, the Antonine Wall, not to keep the Romans in but to keep the Caledonians out and to mark the limit of their imperial control.

Bridei mac Bili

Bridei mac Bili was born into a fractured and treacherous world. The Anglo-Saxon Kingdom of Northumbria had expanded its territory. The Northumbrians ruled by the sword and the cross. Its kings were Christians, and bishops were actively converting pagan and animist peoples north of the Forth. This was the height of Northumbria's power; for a while, it seemed unstoppable.

Bridei's origins remain obscured, but it is safe to conclude that he was far from a mere commoner. He was the son of Bili, the king of the British kingdom of Alt Clut (later known as Strathclyde). His grandfather might have been Nechtan nepos Uerb, a Pictish king who reigned during the late 6th century CE. Some sources also claim that his mother was the daughter of Edwin of Northumbria. These familial ties suggest that Bridei had connections to both the Picts and the powerful Northumbrians, giving him a strong claim to leadership.

His time to shine came when the king of the Northern Picts of Fortriu (a key Pictish kingdom in what is now northern Scotland), Drest mac Donuel, led a failed rebellion against the Northumbrians in 671. He was deposed, and the throne was given to Bridei. Some historians suggest King Ecgfrith himself (who was also his cousin) might have helped him rise to power.

Bridei is remembered for uniting the Pictish tribes, which was far from easy; the Picts were known to be extremely independent and stubborn. Yet, perhaps through a combination of diplomacy, charisma, and force, Bridei succeeded in doing so. He not only displayed his might among those in his territory but also worked on expanding his authority beyond Fortriu. From here on, Bridei was seen as a serious threat by the Northumbrians.

In 685, King Ecgfrith of Northumbria led an invasion into Bridei's territory. Confident after achieving so many previous victories, the king believed that Bridei and his forces could be brought to heel. It was said that his advisors felt uneasy when the campaign was launched. Cuthbert, who had just been made bishop of Lindisfarne, urged caution, but Ecgfrith pushed forward, crossing the Forth River into Pictish territory.

The two forces soon faced each other at Dun Nechtain (near modern-day Dunnichen in Angus) on May 20th, 685. Bridei made use of the landscape. The terrain was hilly and surrounded by marshes and forests. It was perfect for an ambush, especially since the Picts were masters of the land; they knew every ridge and bog.

By feigning retreat, Bridei was able to lure the Northumbrians into an ambush. When the signal came, Pictish warriors came pouring in from the trees. The warriors attacked fast and used the local terrain to pin the Northumbrians against the marsh. King Ecgfrith tried to rally his men but failed. Arrows filled the air, and spears and blades came in direct contact with flesh. It was a massacre. Even King Ecgfrith himself fell in the chaos, his body later transported by Bridei to Iona for burial.

Northumbrian influence in the north became a thing of the past. Bridei reigned for more than two decades. He was said to have encouraged religious growth, built alliances, and laid the groundwork for a more centralized Pictish state, a feat rarely achieved before or after. Even the early Christian chronicler Adomnán, Abbot of Iona, spoke highly of Bridei, noting both his strength and influence.

The Black Douglas: Loyal Companion and a Fearsome Fighter

When people think of Scotland's fight for independence, their minds immediately turn to Robert the Bruce. He was known by many as an outlaw-turned-king, the warrior of Bannockburn, and the man who defied the English Crown. His story has been told and retold countless times.

However, Robert the Bruce did not rise to power alone. He had a loyal companion by his side, whose name is often overlooked. Known as the Black Douglas, he was the one who fought by his side and supported his every decision, long after most had given up.

Sir James Douglas (third from left), alongside the other leaders of
the Wars of Scottish Independence.'

Before earning his feared moniker, he was known simply as Sir James Douglas. Born into Scottish nobility around 1286, he was the son of William Douglas of Douglas, a loyal supporter of the Scottish Crown. When war broke out with England, William's loyalty cost him dearly; his lands were seized by Edward I, and he died in English custody around 1298.

Though James was the rightful heir, the English refused to recognize his claim. As a young man, he found himself landless and legally excluded because he was a Scot in the eyes of a hostile English regime. Attempts to seek legal redress were denied. According to tradition, he was told plainly that he would have nothing unless he lived under English law. With no home, no inheritance, and no justice, James Douglas chose the path of resistance.

He did not hesitate to join Robert the Bruce when he crowned himself king in 1306. The act was seen as an open defiance against English rule and would certainly bring brutal consequences. The situation in Scotland at that time was chaotic, to say the least. Its nobles had scattered, with some turning their backs and swearing allegiance to the English Crown. The people were starving, and Bruce himself was on the run, having been excommunicated by the Catholic Church and defeated in open battle. It was a time when hope was disappearing. Many believed the Scottish cause was coming to an end.

James Douglas, however, believed otherwise. He remained by Bruce's side and waged guerrilla wars against English occupation for years. He succeeded in proving his worth not just as a fierce swordsman but also as a talented tactician. His knowledge of the terrain, surprise, and psychological warfare made him lethal.

The most famous episode involving Douglas came in 1307. He planned on attacking the English garrison stationed at his ancestral home, Douglas Castle. With the help of a local farmer, Douglas and a small band of men managed to remain out of sight until the morning of Palm Sunday. The opportunity to strike came when the soldiers left their stations to attend church. Without wasting a second, Douglas led his men into the church and attacked the English soldiers, who were caught off guard. A brutal fight ensued. Douglas and his men killed as many as they could and took the rest as prisoners. They then threw the bodies into the wine cellar, poured fuel, and set the entire place in flames. Douglas also ordered the wells to be poisoned. This episode, which became known as the Douglas Larder, seemed barbaric, but Douglas was living in a savage time when violent acts were common in a fight for independence.

His reputation grew. The English soldiers feared him so much that they referred to him as the Black Douglas, largely because of his aggressiveness and merciless attacks. While the English hated him, the Scots held Douglas in high esteem. He was known among his countrymen not for cruelty but for his courage and ambition. While other Scottish nobles ran to the other side, Douglas held his ground and protected his homeland. This loyalty earned him another name: the Good Sir James.

Sir James Douglas remained loyal to Robert the Bruce even after Bruce died in 1329. Before dying, Bruce expressed his final wish. He wanted his heart to be taken to the Holy Land so that he could fulfill the crusade he had never lived to make. Of course, the task of carrying it fell to his most important right-hand man, Douglas. It was said that upon breathing his last, Bruce's heart was carefully removed from his chest and embalmed. It was then placed in a silver casket worn around Douglas's neck.

With a small company of knights, Douglas embarked on a journey to the Holy Land to fulfill Bruce's final wish. On his way, Douglas stopped at Spain, where he joined the Christian forces of King Alfonso XI of Castile fighting against the Moors. For the last time, Douglas fought in battle. He charged against the Moors at the Battle of Teba and died a hero. Legend has it that before dying, Douglas tore the casket from his neck and flung it ahead of him as he shouted, "Lead on, brave heart, just as you always did, and I, Douglas, will follow you, or die trying!"

His body was retrieved by his grieving men, and his bones were brought back to Scotland and laid to rest at St. Bride's Church in Douglas. Robert the Bruce's heart was also recovered and buried at Melrose Abbey.

The tomb of Sir James Douglas in St Bride's Kirk.[5]

To this day, statues of Robert the Bruce can be found to commemorate his contributions to the nation. However, Sir James Douglas was rarely spoken of. Yet, without him, there may have been no crown, no victory at Bannockburn, and no final journey for the king's heart. This was the story of a man who lost everything—his name, his land, and his bloodline—and still gave everything he had for the dream of a free Scotland.

Chapter 3 – The Women Behind the Banner

The pain was unbearable. When news of her son's death reached her ears, Lady Finella felt like her whole world had suddenly turned dark. It was the kind of pain, she probably thought to herself, that was worse than anything caused by a blade or an arrow. You could heal these kinds of wounds with stitches and bandages, but the pain of losing someone you loved dearly would never truly heal, no matter the time.

Finella felt sorrow, but she was also angry. Details of her son's death remain unclear. We are not even sure of his name. The 14th-century historian John of Fordun suggested that the reigning king at the time, Kenneth II, killed him in battle. If this were true, it would not be surprising. Kenneth II, despite his efforts to instill law and order, was described as rather ruthless when it came to punishing those who misbehaved. It is said that the king once had thirty people hanged from a tree for stealing.

Finella made it her ultimate mission to ensure the killer of her son paid the price. However, the lady did not act hastily. She walked the grounds in silence and listened to everything. Then came rumors that the king was growing bolder. He had reigned for slightly over two decades. He had slain his rivals, passed many reforms, and even tried to change the very nature of kingship in Scotland. It was acceptable for the throne to be passed between branches of the royal line, but Kenneth was not content with that. He wanted to secure the crown for his own direct bloodline; in other words, he wanted to start a father-son succession rule. Of course, this did not sit well with everyone in court, particularly with his rivals, Constantine III (who was also his cousin) and Gryme (possibly another name for Kenneth III). These two were believed to have plans to get rid of Kenneth II. It is plausible that Finella knew of this coup, but she did not care for their ambitions. She simply wanted the king's head for what he had done to her son. An eye for an eye.

The opportunity came when Kenneth and his small retinue embarked on a royal hunt in the wooded hills near Fettercairn. This was close to where Lady Finella lived. She eventually found him resting beneath the trees. Born into nobility herself—Finella was the daughter of Cuncar, Earl of Angus—the lady was well-versed in the rituals expected in the presence of a king. After approaching the king slowly, she bowed low. After offering the proper courtesies, she lifted her gaze and spoke.

"I have heard words about a conspiracy, Your Majesty," she may have said to Kenneth. "Perhaps it is better for us to speak privately, for even the trees could betray us,"

The king dismissed his guards and, without hesitation, followed Lady Finella through the mossy paths that led to her estate. Here stood a quiet cottage surrounded by Mother Nature. The structure was once used for feasting in autumn and storing wine in winter. Now, it would be used for another purpose. Lady Finella had already made the preparations days, if not months, in advance.

Inside was a statue, which immediately caught the attention of the unsuspecting king. Sensing his curiosity, Lady Finella encouraged the king to touch it. Little did he know that the statue was a trap. The lady had installed strings that connected the statue with a number of concealed crossbows. The moment Kenneth laid his hand on the statue, something creaked. The crossbows released their bolts, finding a target in the king's flesh. He probably staggered at first, but with bolts piercing his body from all sides, the king could not let out a single noise. Blood curdled in his mouth, and some began flowing to the old wooden floor.

Some said Finella did not remain in the cottage to watch him let out his last breath. The lady had already made a headstart, escaping into the woods. The guards eventually found the king in his own pool of blood. They then spread through the woods on horseback, trying to locate the treacherous Lady of the Mearns. They never found her, so they burned her estate to the ground.

Finella had made her way to the cliffs near Fettercairn. Some said she looked back only once before leaping over the waterfall to her death. Others claimed that Finella managed to evade the pursuers and eventually fled to Ireland. Another version said that Finella was, in fact, conspiring with both Constantine III and Gryme. According to this story, she managed to escape through the woods and reunited with the other two conspirators. What happened afterward, though, is rather murky.

Lady Finella was never mentioned in any sort of records after this point, so her fate remains unknown. The place where she was said to have leapt from became known as Den Finella.

As for the throne, Scotland saw the rise of Constantine III as their new king following Kenneth's death. However, Constantine III would soon be killed by Gryme, who wore the crown as Kenneth III. The bloodshed continued. Kenneth II's grandson, Malcolm II, would later kill Kenneth III at the Battle of Monzievaird in 1005. He claimed the throne and ruled until 1034.

Agnes of Dunbar, the Lady Who Held Her Ground.

Agnes was standing at the parapet, her keen eyes observing the English army down below. They seemed restless, though their siege engines were silent for now; in fact, they had remained idle for weeks. Then, her focus shifted to a figure pacing the ground. His name was William Montague, Earl of Salisbury. He was the one commanding the English troops right outside her walls. Even the commander himself was clearly chafing with impatience. Their supplies were wearing thin, and so was their morale.

Agnes looked at the army with a straight expression. Perhaps she did feel a small sense of amusement, but not once did she crack a smile. Her gleaming eyes, however, were enough to needle at English pride.

A depiction of Lady Agnes and her servants standing on top of the walls of Dunbar Castle.[6]

Agnes was the wife of Patrick, 9th Earl of Dunbar and March. Partrick had left the castle months prior after King David II summoned him. He left the safety of the castle in the hands of Agnes.

Many would assume that with only a small force of defenders and a woman who had never held a sword, let alone fought in battles, that Dunbar Castle would easily fall into the hands of the enemy. Perhaps it would have been easier to just hand the keys to the English so that bloodshed could be avoided. However, the countess had no intention of surrendering. After all, she was the daughter of Thomas Randolph, 1st Earl of Moray, who once rode with Robert the Bruce. Courage was a natural trait. Yes, she had never ridden into battle before, but her entire life up to this point was surrounded by men of war. The countess was a keen observer, and she had seen times when victory belonged not to the strongest sword but to the sharpest mind.

The siege began in January 1338. The castle's location was strategic. It stood firmly on a rocky outcrop overlooking the North Sea. It guarded the eastern coastline and the routes into Lothian. Its gates were flanked by basalt cliffs, which provided natural defenses. Having the castle in English hands would definitely strengthen their foothold in the east. And with Patrick away, it should be simple.

Almost immediately, the countess of Dunbar proved them wrong. She commanded what men she had. This small but well-organized force of defenders was likely loyal retainers of the earl of Dunbar. They would have been stationed there before Patrick left to support King David II. Agnes and the men there planned out the defenses and calculated rations. They showed no signs of surrender.

The English first tried negotiation, perhaps with a mix of threats. They told her to surrender peacefully. In return, the English promised mercy to the people behind the walls and wealth and titles for Agnes. The countess was not moved by this. She sent back a polite refusal and ordered the portcullis (a type of heavy iron gate typically found in medieval castles) lowered.

The offense began. The English brought out their catapults and mangonels, siege engines that hurled rocks at the castle's walls. They were confident that Dunbar would soon surrender. Agnes made another appearance on the parapets, but it was not to voice her surrender. Accompanying her were her maids and servants, who carried white handkerchiefs in their hands. The English were confused at first. The maids then dusted the ramparts clean and mockingly curtsied toward the English camp. By that point, it is safe to assume that the English were no longer confused. They cursed the Scots inside.

William Montague ordered the bombardment to be resumed. The English then brought out their battering ram, which they referred to as the "sow." This huge siege engine was designed to destroy the castle gates while shielding the men operating it.

Suddenly, though, they heard the voice of the countess shouting from high up the walls.

"Be careful, my good sirs. Your sow is about to farrow."

A second later, a boulder dropped on the battering ram, smashing it apart. The English soldiers scrambled from its broken structure, fearing that they would die by their own weapon.

This was not the last time that Agnes would mock her enemy. She often came up on the ramparts to call out to the English whenever their attempt to break through her walls failed.

With his patience growing thin as time passed, Montague chose a different attempt to break the countess's spirit. They captured her brother, John Randolph. If Agnes refused to surrender, her brother would die. Her response left the commander speechless.

"I care for my country more than I care for my brother, Sir Montague," she may have said. "After all, he is not all I have. I do have more brothers. And if you kill him, his land and wealth would be mine. In the end, the benefit belongs to me."

John Randolph was spared, though he would later perish in the Battle of Neville's Cross.

The English did everything they could think of. They tried bribing one of her guards. Unbeknownst to them, Agnes had already told her men to accept the payment and then lure the English into a trap.

Five months had passed since the siege began, and the English could not say they had made progress. Taking the castle by force was definitely out of the question. The morale of their troops was decreasing, and their food supply was also dwindling. They could no longer bear to wake up each day with the sight of Agnes and her maids brushing off the dust on the damaged stonework with their white handkerchiefs.

Dunbar Castle ruins in 1987.[7]

King Edward III was becoming increasingly unhappy about the cost of maintaining the siege. It cost the English nearly six thousand pounds, which is roughly equivalent to £5 million to £10 million today. Montague was left with no choice but to lift the siege and retreat. Agnes had won.

Stories of her defending Dunbar spread across the land. They called her Black Agnes. While some accounts suggest the nickname was given to reflect her fierce and headstrong traits, others claimed it came from her dark complexion and black hair.

Isabella MacDuff

It was March 25th, 1306, and Scotland was again plunged into a period of uncertainty. Robert the Bruce had declared himself king, but this was only the beginning of the chaos. A few weeks earlier, Robert was said to have committed one of the most shocking acts in Scottish history. He had slain John III Comyn, Lord of Badenoch and his rival to the throne, on the altar of the Greyfriars Church in Dumfries. Some viewed his act as a bold move, while others condemned it, especially since Robert chose to spill blood on holy ground.

As a result, Bruce was excommunicated. Despite being cut off from the Catholic Church, Bruce refused to back down. He arranged his coronation at Scone Abbey, which was the traditional site of Scottish coronation ceremonies. One problem arose, though. According to tradition, only a member of the MacDuff family, the earls of Fife, had the ancient right to place the crown on the king's head. Unfortunately for Bruce, the current earl of Fife favored Edward I of England. So, it was not surprising when he outright refused to attend the coronation.

Isabella MacDuff changed the course of history. She was married to John Comyn, Earl of Buchan (not to be confused with the Comyn that Bruce had slain earlier). This John Comyn was not only one of Bruce's greatest enemies but also a staunch supporter of the English Crown. Isabella, however, did not share her husband's loyalty. Despite knowing the risk—there was a strong possibility of her being intercepted, imprisoned, or even killed for treason—Isabella made the journey south.

She succeeded in crossing the war-torn lands and arrived at Scone. She was not the first to arrive; Bruce and his supporters were already there. In fact, the coronation had taken place the day before (on March 25th). Bruce was crowned by a representative of Clan MacDuff. But a representative was not enough. Without a MacDuff, the ceremony felt incomplete. This was where Isabella played a role.

On March 27th, 1306, a second coronation ceremony was held. This time, Isabella placed the crown on Robert the Bruce's head. He was now a king by ancient custom, sanctioned by the hand of a MacDuff, as had been done for generations. With the church having excommunicated Bruce for the murder of John Comyn and many Scottish nobles still undecided or opposed, this public gesture by Isabella gave his claim a powerful sense of legitimacy.

Isabella MacDuff crowning Robert the Bruce at Scone.[8]

However, her choice to crown him came at a cost. King Edward I of England was furious after hearing about it. A defiant MacDuff—and a woman at that—had crowned his enemy. This was not just treason but also a personal insult to the English king. When Bruce's forces suffered a major defeat at Methven in June 1306, King Edward turned his attention to the very woman who had meddled in the affair.

Although Robert the Bruce sent Isabella away, along with his queen (Elizabeth de Burgh), their daughter Marjorie, and his sisters, the English would soon get what they sought. After being betrayed by William II, Earl of Ross, Isabella and the other women were captured. Edward then ordered a punishment designed to humiliate Isabella, turning her into an example for the public. She was locked in a wooden cage that was reinforced with iron. The cage was suspended from the walls of Berwick Castle. Not only was Isabella exposed to the harsh weather, but she was also placed in full view of the townspeople. Food was delivered daily to keep her alive. She was guarded but otherwise left alone.

She lived in this cage for four years. She grew accustomed to the townspeople gathering to gawk at her. Some threw insults for betraying the English Crown, while others had a small glimmer of pity in their eyes. But not once did Isabella MacDuff regret her decisions. Attempts to secure her release were made by Sir Robert Keith and Sir John Mowbray to no avail.

She remained in the cage even after the death of Edward I. It was only in 1310 that she was removed from the cage and transferred to the Carmelite friary at Berwick. The decision to relax her punishment was not necessarily an act of kindness or compassion. Some suggest Bruce was gaining support and becoming more powerful. Isabella MacDuff was seen as a valuable hostage. The English knew that she could be used as leverage and that it would be unwise for them to allow her to die from mistreatment.

Isabella was also said to have been transferred once more in 1313, though the location remains a mystery. From here on, her name disappears from the records. Bruce's female relatives were allowed to return to Scotland in early 1315, but Isabella's name was not included in the records, suggesting that she had probably died by then.

Lady Anne Mackintosh

The sharp knocks on the door startled her. Anne Mackintosh sprang to her feet and walked to the door of Moy Hall. Her breath was controlled, though she could feel her heartbeat growing faster with each passing second. When she opened the door, she was hastily greeted by a courier.

"They are on the march, my lady," the courier said, almost out of breath. "Lord Loudoun, his men..." He stopped to take a breath. "They are coming to seize the prince come morning,"

Lady Anne gave a simple nod. The courier was puzzled by her lack of panic, but at the same time, he knew the lady had already strategized a plan long before he journeyed to her estate.

Lady Anne Farquharson of Invercauld had been raised in the thick forests of Braemar. Her father was a staunch Jacobite. Even when she was a young girl, Anne was exposed to the stories about the exiled

Stuarts and the royal birthright they believed had been usurped. So, it was not surprising to see where her loyalty stood. Like her father and others who had Farquharson blood running through their veins, Lady Anne was a Jacobite, through and through.

A portrait of Lady Anne Mackintosh.[9]

Ironically, Anne was married to Angus Mackintosh, a Hanoverian officer. He served as a captain in Lord Loudon's regiment and fought at the Battle of Falkirk Muir in 1746. However, Anne bowed to no man's allegiance, not even her husband's.

When Charles Edward Stuart (better known as Bonnie Prince Charlie) returned to Scotland in 1745 to claim his father's throne, Anne was among the first to show her support. The time was perfect too; her husband was away commanding government troops, giving her an opportunity to rally the support of his clan.

Although Angus aligned with the Hanoverians, not everyone in Clan Mackintosh shared the same loyalty. The clan had a history of Jacobite sympathies. Many of the clan's members, especially from allied families like the MacGillivrays, still leaned toward the Stuart cause. It was not difficult for Anne to raise them for the Jacobite cause. Records estimate that Anne managed to gather between two hundred and eight hundred men from Clan Mackintosh and the confederation of Clan Chattan.

Confidence was always Anne's strongest suit. With the support of these men, she sent words to the prince, offering her husband's warriors. It was said that the prince held her in high esteem, calling her "La Belle Rebelle," which means "the beautiful rebel."

To ensure the Jacobite cause did not falter, Lady Anne knew she had to protect the prince. When news of the advancement of Loudon's men arrived, Anne immediately chose five men to carry out her plans. She gave each of them a torch and a task. They were ordered to ride into the night and approach Lord Loudoun's camp from different directions, though not directly. She was not planning to clash with the massive troops but rather to mislead them.

Positioned in different directions, these five men then banged drums, fired pistols, and fiercely shouted their clan's battle cries. They made it sound as if an entire Jacobite army was lying in wait.

The ruse worked. They made use of the rolling hills, so the sound of footsteps, battle cries, and pistols firing gave the illusion of a much larger force preparing to attack. It also did not help that the ruse was made at night when visibility was poor and nerves were high. Plus, the government troops were already wary of Jacobite ambushes. Any noise or shadow they witnessed at night could easily be perceived as something far greater than it was. The English, startled from their sleep, chose to retreat.

The prince slept undisturbed in Moy Hall that night, unaware of how close he had come to capture. It is said, though no records confirm it, that Charles awoke to a warm fire and a simple breakfast. After serving oatcakes and eggs, Anne, almost offhandedly, informed him of the incident that took place in the night.

Soon, the prince advanced on the lightly defended Inverness, which fell with little resistance. Among the prisoners taken was none other than

Captain Angus Mackintosh. However, he was not punished severely. Instead, the prince paroled the captain into the custody of his own wife. It is said that when Angus was brought to Moy Hall, Lady Anne welcomed him with warmth.

"Your servant, Colonel," Angus said to her wife as he bowed.

Anne then replied, "Your servant, Captain."

This very exchange was where her nickname, Colonel Anne, came from.

However, glory was not meant to last for the Jacobites. Their hopes were crushed at Culloden Moor on April 16th, 1746. Many fell on the battlefield, including those rallied by Anne. She was arrested and subjected to house arrest, where she remained under the supervision of her mother-in-law.

Anne's name did not disappear from the records after this. She was said to have been involved in a certain episode involving Anne McKay, a local Inverness woman who was to be whipped through the streets. Her crime was simply aiding the escape of a Jacobite officer. Viewed as a crime in the eyes of the government, Lady Anne saw it as an honorable act of loyalty. So, she did not hesitate to step in and stop the punishment.

Another episode that mentioned her name took place years later. Lady Anne and her husband attended a social event in London, where Prince William, Duke of Cumberland—the very man who had crushed the Jacobites at Culloden—was also in attendance. He asked Anne to dance, choosing a pro-government tune. The lady complied politely. Then, when it was her turn to choose, she requested a Jacobite tune. Caught in the trap of courtesy, the prince was left with no choice but to accept.

Anne Mackintosh eventually died on March 2nd, 1787, in Leith, the harbor district of Edinburgh. Although few outside Scotland have heard of her, Lady Anne Mackintosh was never forgotten. She was buried in a grave that has two items to honor her memory. One is a white Jacobite rose, a symbol of her undying support for the Jacobite cause, and the other is a commemorative plaque that keeps her story alive.

Chapter 4 – Union Without Celebration

Word travels fast. Queen Elizabeth I of England had breathed her last, leaving the throne vacant. This meant only one thing: James VI, King of Scots, would soon ride south.

Some in the taverns were already clinking their mugs, speaking of what this could mean. A Scottish king wearing two crowns? Surely that must be a sign of favor, perhaps a step closer toward prosperity. Others, however, were not so sure. Scotland had long been treated as the lesser of the two kingdoms. Surely the English would not change their minds so suddenly.

This was not the first time a king sat on two thrones. The world knew the story of Charles V, who ruled both Spain and the Holy Roman Empire. He had stretched his reach across continents, balancing power between distant realms. Some would agree that Charles governed deliberately, always returning to remind his people that he belonged to all of them, not the other way around.

James, on the other hand, seemed like he was about to do something different. Even before the messengers from England reached Edinburgh to deliver news of the queen's passing, James had already ensured preparations were underway. It was as if his mind had already crossed the border before his body even did. Courtiers were jostling for a place in his train. They were well aware that once James departed south, influence would flow from London, not Edinburgh.

It is safe to conclude that the air in Edinburgh shifted on the day King James left for England. There was neither celebration nor mourning in Edinburgh. Market stalls remained open, but voices were hushed. Church bells rang, but not for a specific ceremony. The city just watched as the wagons were loaded and servants hurried through the palace grounds, their hands full of scrolls, silverware, and other items that once filled the halls of Scottish royalty. In a matter of days, these items would adorn the corridors of Whitehall Palace.

Most Scots wondered what it meant to have a kingdom without a king. James would still be their monarch in name and law, but he would not be physically present. He had promised the Scots that he would return to Edinburgh every three years. The king eventually broke his promise; he only returned once, briefly in 1617, to mark the fiftieth anniversary of his accession (he was crowned king of Scots at the age of thirteen months).

En Route to Becoming James I of England

There was never a doubt that Queen Elizabeth would leave behind a complicated legacy. She passed away at Richmond Palace in March 1603. She left no child, so there was no official heir to the throne. The late queen never married, despite being introduced to numerous suitors; her decision to remain unmarried earned her the nickname the Virgin Queen. Still, even without a male figure by her side, her long reign kept England stable, Protestant, and powerful. But now with her death, the English stood at a crossroads. Everyone in the kingdom had the same question: who would wear the crown?

Some thought England would remain without a monarch, at least for a short while, because the queen had not named her successor. However, the answer came faster than they expected. The throne was to be passed to a Scot, a man who, until then, never set foot on English soil.

To those unfamiliar with royal bloodlines, it seemed a surprising choice. Scotland and England had fought like divided siblings forced to share a house. For centuries, these two kingdoms were entangled in a rather complex relationship. They traded goods but also exchanged insults, invaded one another, and agreed to uneasy truces. The border had been drawn and redrawn with blood, and peaceful alliances were usually broken in a matter of years, if not months. And yet, in the end, it was James whom they turned to. Of course, this was not out of affection but out of necessity.

James was the great-great-grandson of Henry VII of England through Margaret Tudor, Henry's eldest daughter. Margaret had married James IV of Scotland, uniting Tudor and Stewart blood. Their descendants, though often tangled in politics and religion, held a legitimate claim to the English throne. And so, James, though Scottish, was family by birth.

However, blood alone was not the sole reason behind James's rise to the throne. For years, the king of Scots had been laying careful foundations. He shone a spotlight on himself, making sure the English were aware of his existence and capabilities. He addressed the English nobles politely in his letters and presented himself as a scholar-king who was well versed in politics and deeply understood the divine right of kings.

In his writings, especially the *Basilikon Doron* (written for his eldest son, Henry, offering advice on how to truly rule a kingdom) and *The True Law of Free Monarchies*, James argued that kings were chosen by God and should rule without interference from Parliament or the people.

Portrait of James I of England. [10]

This belief in divine right appealed to many in England, particularly those wary of political chaos or religious unrest. Even Elizabeth I claimed she was God's anointed ruler and expected obedience. But it is worth noting that the English tradition had long expected that a king would rule alongside Parliament, not above it. So, while they accepted divine right in principle, they were far less willing to accept a monarch who ignored their privileges or demanded obedience without question.

Interestingly enough, even Elizabeth left signs that James was her preferred successor. Of course, the queen made no formal declaration, perhaps fearing antagonizing rival claimants or encouraging rebellion. It could be plausible that her most trusted officials were made aware of this. The secretary of state, Robert Cecil, was said to have been in contact with James for years, quietly managing correspondence and coordinating the transition. When the time finally came, messengers were already halfway to Edinburgh. James received the news at Holyrood and, within days, accepted the call. He crossed the border just after Easter.

However, no matter how smooth the transition was, deep contradictions existed. For England, the hope was that James would be English enough. They hoped their new king would be more than willing to adopt their customs, politics, and court. James did not see himself as a mere successor to Elizabeth. He saw himself as a unifier, the first ruler of a new, united realm.

While the situation in Edinburgh was dim as the king was leaving, his arrival in England was celebrated. He was greeted warmly by English officials at Berwick. Cathedral bells rang to mark his ascension to the throne. Everywhere he stepped, there were pageants, feasts, and floral arches straining under their own symbolism.

James knew first impressions were important. So, he made sure to play his part well. He dined, smiled, and listened to the flattery thrown by his new subjects. He blended both piety and self-assurance in his speeches. To the crowds, he spoke of union and peace. To the mayors and magistrates, he spoke of law and order. To the nobles, he spoke of lineage and divine right. He ensured each audience received the version of James they wished to see, at least for a while.

There were neither garlands nor feasts in Edinburgh—only the sense that something important was now missing. The palace gates remained closed, and the chapel was awfully quiet. The king's name still appeared on legal documents and proclamations, but that was about it. His presence was never felt. What followed afterward was not outright chaos but a drift.

The most obvious change was the missed appointments. Although Holyrood Palace remained a royal property, it slowly lost its function as the nucleus of political life. Gone were the days when meetings filled the chambers of Holyrood. At first, those who remained tried to keep things going. The Privy Council met, though with diminished authority. Clerks arrived to draft documents, though fewer required signing. James's absence made direct appeals more difficult, and petitions often went unanswered.

The king of Scots took no official step to dismantle the Scottish court when he departed for London. There was no decree announcing its closure, nor was any law dissolved. However, like a theater without an audience, its purpose quietly disappeared in his absence.

The change was not only felt by the nobles and those who worked at the palace. The king's absence also affected the kingdom's economy. The goldsmith who had once supplied filigree buckles for the royal wardrobe now focused on crafting mundane items like communion cups. The printer who had worked on proclamations turned to almanacs and ballads. The weavers who once supplied fine linen for the palace found themselves stitching kerchiefs for merchants' wives.

Of course, even the rhythm of Edinburgh changed. Months ago, feast days brought color and music to the streets, but now, they passed with little notice. Without a royal presence, there were no processions winding through the closes (narrow alleyways). No fireworks filled the dark sky, and no grand banquets were thrown to welcome nobles and chiefs from clans all over the kingdom. Although celebrations were still held every once in a while, they were quieter. More often than not, they were organized by guilds or parishes rather than the palace.

However, Scotland was still a kingdom. Its Parliament still met, the Kirk (the Church of Scotland) still governed, and its laws remained its own. On paper, nothing had changed. Power had not disappeared; it was just relocated. It now pulsed from Whitehall, not Edinburgh. Scotland had become a kingdom with a king who lived outside its borders.

While James was celebrated and welcomed when he first set foot in England, this was nothing more than an illusion. It would crack once he began to govern. Those far from the palace and Parliament cheered and praised their new monarch, but courtiers, ministers, and nobles quickly grew wary, especially when James, despite sitting on a throne in England, surrounded himself with Scots.

The king did not travel to England alone. He brought a retinue of familiar faces. His advisors, gentlemen of the bedchamber, and household staff were the same ones who had served him in Edinburgh and Stirling. Of course, it was only natural that he brought his own circle to his new palace, but this stirred discontent among many of the English nobles. Somehow, they felt like it was an invasion. Queen Elizabeth had kept a tight court that was fiercely English in tone and temperament. But when James arrived, in just a matter of weeks, Whitehall was filled with foreign accents and surnames unfamiliar to Englishmen.

English courtiers who had waited patiently for advancement under Elizabeth now found themselves overlooked in favor of men they considered outsiders. In their eyes, the Scots were grasping or perhaps, in a harsher depiction, greedy. They were too forward with their petitions and lacked shame in seeking favor. Of course, some of the resentment was purely political. James was not completely familiar with English parliamentary custom. Back in Scotland, the king held more direct authority, and the Scottish Parliament was more easily influenced by the Crown. This was not the case with England. James underestimated just how tightly the House of Commons guarded its privileges. While he expected obedience, they expected negotiation. James also often spoke of uniting England and Scotland into one, though many Englishmen were uncomfortable with the idea. Despite having the king of Scots sitting on their throne, they still did not like the idea of treating Scotland as their equal.

There were subtler frictions too. The English court had long prized refinement, caution, and control. Elizabeth I, for one, was known to have turned hesitation into an art form. She delayed decisions and was deliberately vague and cautious, especially when it came to important matters such as alliances and war. This was not a sign of weakness. She turned hesitation into a political tool. By not giving quick answers, she kept people guessing, maintained control over her court and suitors, and avoided making enemies too soon. James, however, was starkly different.

James was a learned man, but he was also more direct, expressive, and informal than what the English elites were used to. He rarely acted as gracefully as the late queen. He spoke candidly, laughed heartily, and drank more freely. His open affection toward certain courtiers stirred gossip among his English subjects. Once he favored someone, the king was said to have showered them with luxurious gifts, titles, and power. This did not change when he lost interest in them, as he rarely revoked what he had granted them.

Interestingly, those he clearly showed fondness for were often attractive and significantly younger men. This led historians to speculate that the king might have been gay or bisexual. The most famous man that the king considered his favorite was George Villiers. Villiers rose from a humble cupbearer through the ranks under James's patronage, eventually becoming the duke of Buckingham. Villiers was the only non-royal to have received a dukedom during his reign. The two also often exchanged letters filled with affection and warmth, which further fueled court rumors.

To the common people, especially in London, the king remained something of a curiosity. He was not disliked, but he was not as loved as Elizabeth had been. He did not walk among his people. He did not dazzle with ceremony.

Although there were mixed feelings about his reign, James still believed his main mission was to unite the two kingdoms. However, the more he reached toward a union, the more resistance he met. England had gained a new monarch, but many did not ask for a new country. By trying to rule both, James was slowly becoming aware that he was fully embraced by neither.

Nevertheless, the king was not known to back down easily. He continued to imagine a single nation, one people under one crown, with shared laws, shared worship, and shared purpose. The king soon introduced a new coin, known as the unite. It featured his profile wearing the imperial crown and holding the orb and scepter, which were thought to be symbols of authority over both realms. The other side of the coin was his newly designed royal arms and the Latin phrase "Faciam eos in gentem unam," which is translated to "I will make them one nation."

James then proposed a new name for the nation, Great Britain, and gave himself the title King of Great Britain. He used the term repeatedly in his speeches and official documents. (The first official ruler of Great Britain was not James, though; it was Queen Anne, who became the ruler of a unified Britain in 1707.) James was also known to be a passionate collector and wearer of jewelry. He commissioned a special jewel to commemorate his rise to the English throne. This gem-encrusted pendant was called the Mirror of Great Britain. And then there was the flag. He commissioned a design that wove together the red cross of Saint George and the white saltire of Saint Andrew (a diagonal X-shaped cross).

King James I and VI wearing the Mirror of Great Britain on his hat.[11]

However, Parliament did not share his vision of a united kingdom. They refused to abandon centuries of law and customs simply because a king declared it so. Even those who respected James found his push for union premature; it was idealistic at best, presumptuous at worst. Englishmen were Englishmen. Scots were Scots. Official seals still bore separate arms, and maps remained unchanged.

Back in Scotland, James's speeches and visions about a union landed flat. His new identity as "King of Great Britain" meant little to the ministers in the Kirk or the traders on the burgh councils. They still lived in a country with its own laws, parliament, and church. But increasingly, it felt like they were living in a country without a voice.

At first, people adjusted. The old court rituals faded. Petitions slowed. Council business became more cautious. Without a monarch to appeal to directly, power began to tilt inward toward the church, local landowners, and factions. But over time, the absence became more than inconvenient. It became corrosive. What troubled many was not that James had gone to London; it was that he began to sound like a man who had forgotten where he came from.

The Scots never saw their king in the flesh ever again, save for the year 1617. James even appointed bishops in Scotland from afar. It became increasingly clear that their king favored men who aligned with his preference for English-style church hierarchy, which undoubtedly did not sit well with many Scots. They remained true to the Presbyterian way. They believed that each church should govern itself without bishops. Despite rising concerns expressed by ministers and church elders during sermons, James turned a deaf ear. He did not listen to the complaints of his own people and held strong to the belief that he was a king chosen by God, giving him the very right to decide what was best.

Although dissatisfaction was obviously growing, there were still ambitious Scots who made the journey south. They hoped to find favor at the English court, where they could feel their king's presence. However, only a few succeeded in making this hope come true. George Home, 1st Earl of Dunbar, for instance, was one of the few Scots who managed to hold influence across England. The majority felt like outsiders the moment they set foot on English soil. The closer one stood to the throne, the more English one was expected to become, and many Scots were not willing to give up their identity.

James ruled over both Scotland and England for twenty-two years, from 1603 until 1625. He died in England, surrounded by English courtiers and buried in English soil. Although the two kingdoms shared the same monarch, James's efforts to achieve a full union were ultimately unsuccessful. He was succeeded by his son, Charles I, who continued to wear both crowns.

Charles, however, preferred a different approach. Where James used gentle persuasion to unite the two kingdoms, Charles tried to force it. Like his father, he did not set foot in Scotland for years and delayed his Scottish coronation. It was only in 1633 that he made his journey north to be crowned in Edinburgh. Although this was the first time in decades that a monarch had returned to Scotland in person, his arrival was far from a joyful reunion. Later on, Charles tried to change how the Scottish Church worshiped, making it more like the English Church. He even went to the extent of introducing a new prayer book without asking the Kirk or the people.

The reaction was, as expected, furious. Protests broke out across the country, and before long, Scotland was at war with its own king. These were known as the Bishops' Wars, and they were just the beginning of a much larger crisis that would spread across Scotland, England, and Ireland. After years of war, rebellion, the king's execution (Charles I was executed in 1649—the only English king to be executed in history), and political chaos, Scotland was finally faced with the question James had raised: should the two kingdoms fully unite?

The Acts of Union united the Parliaments of Scotland and England into the Kingdom of Great Britain in 1707. However, the union was not the result of widespread public support but rather political and economic pressures. It was simply a union of governments instead of a true union of the people. In the years that followed, discontent simmered beneath the surface, eventually erupting in the Jacobite rebellions. These uprisings sought to restore the old order and reject the union that the majority of the Scots had never truly accepted.

Chapter 5 – Stone and Specter

Mists, green slopes, endless rolling hills, bagpipes, and kilts are not the only things that are synonymous with Scotland. When people think of the nation, one of the first images that comes to mind is a castle. Some conjure an enormous castle perched high on a cliff, while others imagine one nestled quietly beside a loch, with thick mist covering part of its crumbling towers.

There is no mistake that castles are woven deeply into the fabric of Scottish identity. They are more than just stone structures; these castles are a treasure trove of the country's turbulent and dramatic past.

The story of Scotland's many castles began in the 12th century when King David I arrived on the scene. He brought sweeping changes to the land, such as feudalism, Norman customs, and the introduction of motte-and-bailey castles. Considered one of the earliest forms of medieval fortification, these castles were quick to build. They were constructed from timber, set stop manmade earth mounds (there were also instances when natural hills were used), and surrounded by defensive ditches. However, Scotland's rugged landscape and brutal political climate demanded something sturdier. By the 13th century, these early fortifications took a change in their form. Stone castles began to rise, complete with thick walls and better fortifications designed to withstand more advanced sieges, fires, and even time itself.

During the Wars of Scottish Independence, these castles played important roles. Think of the famous Stirling Castle or even Edinburgh Castle. In addition to serving as military strongholds, these castles were also strategic prizes hotly contested by the Scots and the English. They were not merely built to house the nobility. These castles were, unsurprisingly, the nerve centers of power, law, and resistance. Suffice it to say that whoever held the castle held the region.

However, by the 17th and 18th centuries, many castles had been abandoned, dismantled, or repurposed. While some noble families adapted castles into grand homes, others simply let them fall into ruin. But still, even in ruins, these castles never disappeared from Scotland's imagination. When the world saw the emergence of the Romantic era (also known as Romanticism), stories of Scotland's castles spread not only across the country but eventually throughout the world. Writers like Sir Walter Scott preserved the stories and myths of these castles. These structures became the stuff of poetry, legend, and even ghost stories.

It is almost inevitable, really. When a building has stood for centuries, witnessing sieges, murders, betrayals, and heartbreak, the imagination fills in what history leaves unsaid. Many of Scotland's castles are as famous for their spectral residents as they are for their architecture. These tales flourished during the 18th and 19th centuries, right alongside the rise of the Gothic novel and Romantic fascination with the supernatural.

Edinburgh Castle, for example, has a story that still sends a chill down the spine of those who hear it today. Legend has it that, back in its glory days, the castle was so large that it had a network of hidden tunnels beneath the ground. Some believe they were constructed for covert purposes. Perhaps they were reserved for the royalty, who would use them as secret escape routes during times of war or political upheaval. The real purpose of the tunnels has never been confirmed, but their rediscovery led to the beginning of a haunting story known as the Ghost Piper of Edinburgh Castle.

Edinburgh Castle.[19]

The story has it that, almost immediately after rediscovering the labyrinthine network, the city's authorities began searching for someone willing to explore the old network. No one had ventured into the tunnels for many years, so not a single person could foresee the dangers that lurked below. Still, curiosity beats anxiety. For unknown reasons, the authorities finally decided to send a young piper into the tunnels. The boy was to navigate the labyrinthine network while playing his pipes. Through his melodies below, those above could roughly trace his position, allowing them to create a map of the tunnels.

The boy delved into the unknown tunnels and played tunes. The melodies resonated through the streets, attracting the attention of nearly everyone near the castle. Some even paused in their daily chores just so they could follow the progress of the piper boy making his way beneath the cobblestone streets.

Suddenly, the lovely tune stopped. The people claimed they heard the last notes near Tron Kirk, a parish church on the Royal Mile. They waited, hoping for the boy to resume playing his melody, but only silence followed. Reports were made to the authorities, who launched a search for the piper boy. However, no trace of him was ever found, not even his bagpipe. He had mysteriously disappeared. Left with no other clues, the authorities sealed the tunnels. While some agreed it was done to prevent another individual from going missing, others whispered they did so to bury the secret of what truly happened to the unfortunate piper.

Of course, the story did not end there. Ever since his disappearance, people have reported that they can sometimes hear the distant sound of bagpipe tunes being played from beneath the streets of Edinburgh, especially near the castle. People have concluded that this music must be played by none other than the spirit of the unfortunate boy, who, even in death, is still searching for a way out of the eerie tunnels.

Of course, the Ghost Piper of Edinburgh Castle is just one of the many eerie tales of Scotland. There is another haunting story, though this one took place in Crathes Castle. Built by Alexander Burnett, the castle features a classic Scottish tower-house design. Construction began sometime in 1553, but the castle did not take its final form until 1596. This delayed completion was largely due to the political turmoil involving Mary, Queen of Scots.

Crathes Castle today.[18]

Interestingly, this story first began not at the castle itself but in a house by a loch, where the Burnetts resided. Legend has it that the young lord, Alexander Burnett, had fallen in love with Bertha, whom many believed to be a distant cousin. Bertha, having been entrusted to their care, temporarily shared the same roof as the Burnetts. However, things took a dark turn when Alexander returned home one day, only to find his lover in bed, clinging to what was left of her life. Alexander was overcome with sorrow. Knowing that Bertha would soon leave him and depart to another world, he reached for a goblet of wine on the table, hoping he could share one last drink with her.

Suddenly, his mother, Lady Agnes, snatched the goblet from his hand and threw it out the window. This was when the truth was revealed. Ever since his father's passing, Alexander has been under the strict supervision of Lady Agnes. She had envisioned Alexander marrying into a noble family, but she knew that Alexander had given his heart to Bertha. Every time Alexander spoke of her, the lady would clearly display her disapproval, hoping he would change his mind. However, seeing that their bond was getting stronger each day, Lady Agnes decided to make a cruel move. She poured wine into a goblet and added poison. The lady then made the unsuspecting Bertha drink it. The plan worked, as Bertha died soon after.

This was not the last time Lady Agnes would see Bertha. Months later, Bertha's father arrived, knocking at their door. He intended to bring his daughter home, but instead, he was welcomed by Lady Agnes, who attempted to explain her sudden death. She then stopped mid-conversation when she felt a bone-chilling cold sweeping through the room. Her eyes widened in terror. Lady Agnes screamed and pointed to a corner of the room, claiming that Bertha had risen from the dead to get her. Consumed by terror, Lady Agnes fell dead to the floor.

The episode never left the Burnetts' memory. Hoping to escape the past, they moved out of their house and into Crathes Castle. However, it seems that leaving behind the ghosts of their past was not possible. On the anniversary of Bertha's death, a spirit referred to by locals as the White Lady emerged at the old house before making a journey to Crathes Castle. While some believed this specter was none other than the soul of Bertha, others suggested that it was actually Lady Agnes, her soul cursed for eternity and denied rest.

Crathes Castle is also the home of the Green Lady. Almost similar to the White Lady, this specter was said to have haunted the castle's rooms and hallways from time to time. Her story is not as detailed as the story of Bertha and Lady Agnes, though. Even her identity remains a mystery. Some say she was a servant girl who fell in love with a nobleman residing at the castle.

Another version suggests she developed a relationship with an unknown stableboy. She eventually got pregnant and gave birth. Many decades later, a shocking discovery was made during a renovation. Workers uncovered the skeletal remains of a woman and a child concealed behind a fireplace. If these remains were indeed hers and her child's, they might have been murdered, their bodies hidden to conceal their fate. They also could have died during childbirth. Many lean toward the possibility of them being victims of murder. If they died during childbirth, their bodies would have been buried properly, not hidden behind a fireplace.

It is said that the Green Lady lingers in the castle to this day. Visitors and staff members often report witnessing her gliding through one corridor to another. There are also those who describe feeling a sense of deep sorrow in the room where her remains were hidden. Others speak of an eerie feeling of being watched and of a distant voice that stops them from entering the room. Some also talk of catching glimpses of a figure in green out of the corner of their eyes. The specter always vanishes the very moment they turn to look directly at it.

Hermitage Castle, Home of a Sorcerer and His Minion

Hermitage Castle is not the kind of medieval castle that lives in your imagination. It does not feature a cylindrical tower topped with a conical roof. It does not have fluttering red banners. Instead, this fortress rose from the earth like a slab of square stone. It is nestled in the wild and lonely landscape of the Scottish Borders, above the Hermitage Water (a river in Liddesdale), and today, the castle looks rather grim and weather-beaten.

What remains of the Hermitage Castle.[14]

The structure's origins trace back to the 13th century. It was first constructed as a motte-and-bailey fortification before being rebuilt in stone by the de Soules family. This was the beginning of the castle's sinister background. William de Soules was a powerful noble. As the lord of Liddesdale, he held favor under King Edward I of England. He remained loyal to the English Crown for slightly over a decade, and as a result, he was rewarded with a knighthood and the lands of Sir Robert Keith, despite them being in the hands of the Scots at that time. However, when Robert the Bruce gained victory at Bannockburn in 1314, Soules sided with the Scots. Four years later, he was made butler of Scotland.

William de Soules was not remembered for his chivalry or battlefield glory. Instead, he gained notoriety for his involvement in dark magic. Stories claimed that he was a sorcerer who communicated with the devil himself. According to folktales, he practiced black magic and human sacrifice. He was believed to have kidnapped his enemies and unfortunate villagers, boiling them alive in a cauldron at nearby Ninestane Rig. He also had a demonic minion known as Robin Redcap to aid him in the realm of dark arts. As these stories spread across the land, terror grew among the locals. Eventually, they rose up and captured him. William de Soules was wrapped in lead and burned alive. His minion, on the other hand, vanished into thin air.

History, though, has a very different story for de Soules. He was said to have been involved in a conspiracy against Robert the Bruce. De Soules was eventually captured and died in prison. This version is more realistic, but the Scots love a good ghost story. Locals claimed to have seen the ghost of William de Soules haunting the corridors of Hermitage Castle. Some reported eerie occurrences when they heard the screams and sobs of his victims being sacrificed. Others spoke of catching a glimpse of a small figure with a blood-red cap, who could possibly be de Soules's minion, Robin Redcap.

Over the centuries, Hermitage Castle passed through several hands, including the Dacres and the Douglases. Hermitage Castle also has a story that involves Mary, Queen of Scots. In 1566, she rode more than twenty-five miles through dangerous terrain to visit James Hepburn, 4th Earl of Bothwell, who lay wounded inside the castle. Not long after, Bothwell became her third husband, and Mary's life took a tragic turn. Some even said her decision to ride to Hermitage was the moment her destiny shifted.

Hermitage Castle was eventually abandoned in the 17th century. Although no sweeping gardens and ornamentation remain today, the castle has become a museum, open for the public to come and visit its grim halls and staircases, where William de Soules once allegedly schemed his next kidnapping.

Ackergill, a Castle Turned Prison

Ackergill Tower (also known as Ackergill Castle) stands near the windswept coast of Caithness. Its tall stone structure seems almost to brace itself against time, history, and weather. Compared to other castles in Scotland, Ackergill may seem more like a fortified house than a typical stronghold. However, do not be fooled by its innocent design. Behind those walls lies one of the country's most tragic tales, one that involved a woman named Helen Gunn.

Ackergill Castle.[15]

Helen was believed to be the daughter of a man named Lachlan Gunn, who lived in Braemore, not far from Ackergill. Helen was known across Caithness for her beauty and gentle heart. One sight of her was enough for a man to fall in love, although many knew she was already betrothed to her cousin, Alexander Gunn. This was unsurprising given that they grew up together; their closeness eventually turned into love. Wedding plans were set in motion. The day was meant to be a joyful celebration until a certain individual came into the picture, thwarting her happiness.

Dugald Keith of Ackergill had once proposed to Helen. She declined firmly yet politely, but Dugald, a man of pride, never forgot the shame that he felt. Over time, this shame turned into anger. He became obsessed with Helen to the point where he decided that if he could not have Helen, then no one could. When news of her marriage reached his ears, Dugald wasted no time in strategizing his move. After gathering a small band of men from the Keith clan, Dugald stormed Braemore. The

Gunns were caught off guard by the attack, resulting in terrible bloodshed. Helen was carried away like a prize.

She was then locked in Ackergill Tower. No one was allowed to visit her. The only time she had human interaction was with Dugald, though this was against her will. He often visited her only to force himself on her. Days turned into weeks. Helen was left alone, grieving and robbed of all hope. She wanted to escape the confinement of the tower and Dugald's cruel treatment. Eventually, she no longer cared if that freedom came at the cost of her own life.

The story goes that Helen managed to make her way to the very top of Ackergill. Some whispered she did so with the help of a sympathetic jailer. She took a deep breath and leapt. Her body was discovered on the rocky ground below, her bones shattered and the blood already dried. Legend has it that she died in the green dress she had worn on what should have been her wedding day, which led to her nickname, the Green Lady.

Ever since the traumatic incident, locals say they see a woman in green wandering through the castle's halls. This apparition never lingers. Her figure will appear just at the edge of someone's vision before vanishing the very moment one turns. Some also claim to have heard faint weeping or footsteps coming from a spot where no one is walking. Cold drafts, flickering lights, and the eerie sensation of being watched are also common experiences for visitors to the castle.

Sanquhar Castle, an Eternal Home for Those Who Have Been Wronged

Located northeast of Dumfries and constructed in the 13th century by Clan Ross, Sanquhar Castle was once a prestigious fortress guarding the routes between the Scottish Borders and the Highlands. In its prime, the castle played host to royal guests such as Mary, Queen of Scots, and James VI of Scotland. It bore witness to the nation's shifting politics.

Then, as the world stepped into the 14th century, ownership of the castle was passed into the hands of the Crichtons, another one of Scotland's most influential families. Their tenure seemed promising at first. The family used their vast wealth to fortify Sanquhar and expand its elaborate chambers. Little did they know that this opulence would eventually become their undoing. The Crichtons overspent to the point of ruin. By the mid-1600s, their debts were so great that they were forced to sell the property to Sir William Douglas, 1st Duke of Queensberry.

Sadly, Douglas had little interest in maintaining the aging fortress. He let it decay, and Sanquhar gradually crumbled into ruins.

However, the name of the castle was never left out of historical records and works of literature. Oral tradition also ensured that Sanquhar would never be forgotten. The most famous tale surrounding the castle is the tale of Marion of Dalpeddar. According to legend, Marion was a beautiful young woman. Her golden hair flowed down her back like precious threads, and her warm smile could melt the heart of even the most battle-hardened knight. She was beloved by the villagers.

The ruins of Sanquhar Castle.[16]

For reasons unknown to this day, Marion suddenly disappeared. Word spread that her disappearance had something to do with one of the lords of Crichton. No one could confirm this suspicion, though, and the rumor eventually died down.

In 1895, John Crichton-Stuart acquired the castle and started the work to restore his ancestors' home. The workers made a grisly discovery. They uncovered the skeleton of a young woman. Its skull even had a few strands of long blonde hair on it.

This reignited the suspicion that Marion had indeed been murdered. Many believe that she had learned something she was not meant to know, or perhaps she had angered the wrong noble with her refusal or defiance. Whatever the cause, the theory goes that she was silenced, and her body was buried in secret. Of course, her spirit never left Sanquhar. Locals often tell stories of her ghost, tall and pale, pacing the eastern stairwell and endlessly wringing her wrists. Some report hearing a soft weeping echo through the halls, particularly at dawn.

She is not the only restless soul said to haunt Sanquhar. The castle is also believed to be the haunting ground of John Wilson, who was wronged in the late 16th century.

Wilson served under a local laird (a minor lord) named Sir Thomas Kirkpatrick, who was constantly in conflict with an ally of the Crichton family, Douglas of Drumlanrig. However, what began as a personal quarrel between the two men quickly took a darker turn when the Crichtons stepped in. Whether out of malice or loyalty to their ally, the Crichtons chose to strike.

Instead of targeting Kirkpatrick directly, they chose to break him by targeting the man who worked for him. They drew up false charges against Wilson. Whether the Crichtons sought to send a message or simply used Wilson to settle a score, their motives were as cold as the stones that made up their castle. Kirkpatrick, knowing that Wilson was innocent, pleaded for his release, though it fell on deaf ears. In the end, Wilson was dragged from his cell and hanged for crimes he never committed.

Wilson's ghost is said to still walk the ruins of Sanquhar, rattling his chains and groaning in grief. Some claim to hear his footsteps in the dark, pacing the grounds, a soul condemned not by his own deeds but by the cruelty of others. His presence, like Marion's, lingers as a reminder that behind every crumbling wall lies not just history but human consequence.

Chapter 6 – Bloodbaths, Betrayal, and Murders

It was 2016, and a team of researchers was just about to make a gruesome discovery. They were exploring the caves along the coast of the Black Isle in the Highlands of Scotland when they noticed what seemed like a grave tucked in a rocky alcove. As they dug deeper and brushed away the dust and soil that covered the centuries-old grave, they unearthed a human skeleton. It was remarkably intact, but its skull told a rather dark story or perhaps a tragedy.

They uncovered a gaping hole in the skull. Upon further examination, the forensic team discovered that the man also had his jaw dislocated and teeth smashed. They suggested the possibility of the man dying after enduring five severe fractures to the head as a result of being hit multiple times by a blunt weapon. The gaping hole was possibly caused by a sharp weapon driven through the front of his skull as he lay on the ground.

Experts suggest the man lived sometime between 430 and 630 CE, placing him in the early medieval period. He was about thirty years of age when he breathed his last and stood about 5'5" (170 centimeters tall). Scholars believe he might have been a Pictish nobleman or even a member of the royal family. This suggestion was made based on the evidence that lay in his bones. A detailed isotopic analysis revealed that he had consumed a high-protein diet. This was uncommon for the time since the early medieval Scots' diet consisted primarily of grains. The commoners had limited access to meat. More often than not, a meat-rich diet was reserved for the upper class.

Apart from his luxurious diet, the man was also buried in an unusual fashion. While commoners were often buried in simple, shallow graves, this man was interred in a cave. Historians suggest this was done for a reason: cave burial might have been a way for the man to be ritually put to rest at the entrance of the underworld. Archaeologists also discovered animal bones close to where he was buried, suggesting a feast was held during his funeral.

But still the mystery remains. Why did the man suffer such extreme wounds?

Of course, this was not the only discovery that pointed to murder. Another skeleton, found at the Scottish Seabird Centre in North Berwick, bore no signs of blunt trauma but had a series of stab wounds. Forensic analysis revealed a lot. The distinct markings on his shoulder blades and arm bones, which were possibly the result of years of repetitive motion, suggest the man was once an archer. There were also four different stab marks found on the skeleton: two on his left shoulder and another two in his ribs. It is plausible that he was stabbed by a dagger with a lozenge-shaped cross-section. Interestingly, this weapon was typically carried by professional fighters, likely men trained in military service.

Coupled with the precise placement of the stabs, scholars arrived at the conclusion that he was the victim of an assassination. Whoever struck the blows had known exactly what he was doing.

It is safe to say that the vast land of Scotland was no stranger to violence. From ancient times to the medieval age and beyond, murder, betrayal, and calculated assassination have been as much a part of the landscape as the mountains and lochs.

The Story of How Kate Barlass Tried to Stop the Assassination of a King

Bloodshed was about to take place on the evening of February 21st, 1437. King James I of Scotland was as ruthless as he was capable. He was a rather complex figure, making it hard to label him simply as a good or bad ruler. After surviving episodes of treachery and imprisonment in the hands of the English, James I's return to Scotland brought the nation to a greater height. But, of course, even the greatest kings in the world were not shielded from criticism. Despite his contributions, King James I was heavily criticized for his political missteps, unpopular decisions, and strained relationships with the English Parliament and the Scottish people.

When he made it his utmost priority to reduce the power of Scotland's rebellious nobles, James I was sealing his own fate. He had his eyes on the Albany Stewarts, who once had massive influence over the land, almost rivaling the Scottish Crown itself. James dismantled them piece by piece. Even the duke of Albany, Murdoch Stewart (who also played a role in the death of James I's brother, David Stewart), was executed. His family was stripped of their lands. The removal of Murdoch gave the king some peace of mind, but it was only temporary.

Murdoch's son-in-law, the earl of Atholl, Walter Stewart (who was also James's uncle), would soon bring about the king's demise. He had once been a close ally of James. In fact, he was one of the court officials who negotiated James's release from the English. However, his ambition ran deep; Walter believed that he was capable of ruling the nation himself.

Walter Stewart did not embark on a mission to eradicate the king alone. The plot was spearheaded by Sir Robert Graham, another former ally of James. Together with the remnants of the Albany faction and other disgruntled nobles, they made a move to strike at King James I, who was resting behind the secure walls of the Blackfriars Monastery in Perth. The king was not alone at that time; he was accompanied by his queen, Joan Beaufort, and a handful of trusted attendants. Yet, this did not stop the assassins.

Using the cover of darkness, Robert Graham and a small group of men sneaked into the monastery. They headed toward the king's chamber. Although the assassins tried to move as quietly as possible, the commotion they made as they moved through the outer hallways alerted Catherine Douglas, one of the queen's ladies-in-waiting. Relying on her instinct that told her trouble would befall the king, Catherine acted quickly. Despite having no weapons in hand, she rushed to the king's chamber. She tried to secure the door, but the bolt bar that secured the king's chamber had been mysteriously removed earlier that day, possibly by the king's chamberlain, Robert Stewart, the grandson of Walter Stewart.

Without hesitation, Catherine thrust both of arms through the iron brackets. She became a living bolt between the attackers and her king.

Unfortunately, this did not stop the assassins. Their strength was too much for Catherine. The men eventually forced the door open, shattering Catherine's arms. She immediately collapsed and screamed at the top of her lungs, as the pain was indescribable.

She had bought the king a few extra seconds, if not minutes, but they were not enough. James desperately tried to escape the pursuers. He made his way to a sewer passage beneath the monastery, hoping to escape through its exit. His heart dropped the moment he remembered that just days earlier, he had ordered the exit sealed off. This was done to prevent his tennis balls from escaping during games. In a last attempt, he hid in the drain.

The assassins soon poured into the sewer and discovered the king. Instead of begging for his life, James was said to have taken a final stand against the assassins. Armed with only a fireplace poker, the king managed to injure one of his attackers. But there were too many of them. Robert Graham inflicted multiple wounds on the king as they fought. Eventually, James was overpowered and killed. He was stabbed sixteen times.

The murder of King James I was not only a shocking episode in the history of Scotland, but his death also marked the beginning of a dark pattern. Believe it or not, he was the first of five Stewart monarchs to have had a violent demise. His son, James II, would gain the throne at the young age of six. He wore the crown for slightly over two decades. He died during a siege when a cannon exploded near where he was standing. Next in line was James III, who met his fate during the Battle of Sauchieburn in 1488 or shortly afterward, possibly after being stabbed by a mysterious man posing as a priest. The next king, James IV, died in combat at Flodden in 1513. In 1587, Mary, Queen of Scots, was publicly beheaded in England.

As for Queen Joan, who was also a target that evening, she managed to escape, although she suffered some wounds. She immediately sent orders to protect her son, James II, in Edinburgh. News of the murder did not entirely surprise the Scottish court, especially since some considered him a tyrant who recklessly attacked the nobility. Catherine Douglas, on the other hand, was remembered for her bravery. She earned the nickname Kate Barlass for her action of barring the door.

However, what happened to her after the incident remains uncertain since there are no surviving records of her. Some spoke of Catherine living the rest of her life with mangled arms, while others claimed she simply vanished into obscurity. As for the conspirators, they were later captured and subjected to terror. Records tell of how they were dragged naked through the streets and poked with red-hot irons. Robert Graham and Walter Stewart were both tortured before being executed.

The Infamous Black Dinner

Just a few years after the assassination of King James I, another act of treachery took place. This time around, it unfurled inside the stone-clad walls of Edinburgh Castle. Infamously known as the Black Dinner, this historical event was so brutal that it later inspired one of the most popular scenes in modern fiction: the Red Wedding in *Game of Thrones*.

In the year 1440, Scotland was again falling into a period of uncertainty. The king who came to the throne after James I was only a child. The real power was held by his regents, particularly Chancellor Sir William Crichton and the Keeper of Stirling Castle, Sir Alexander Livingston. Together, these men worked to maintain their grip on authority, no matter the cost.

Their biggest threat came from the Douglas family. This rival clan had grown so powerful that the regents feared they would eventually rival that of the monarchy itself, threatening their own influence across the land. At that time, the family was under the leadership of William Douglas, 6th Earl of Douglas. He was only sixteen years old and had recently inherited the title from his father. William Douglas was supported by his younger brother, David. Despite being young, they were popular among the Scottish population. After all, they had forged powerful alliances with other noble families.

It was only a matter of time before they could tip the scales of power. But neither Crichton nor Livingston planned to let that happen. The regents began planning a trap to end the influence of the Douglas brothers. Drawing them straight into battle would plunge Scotland into more turmoil. So, they chose a subtle lure. They invited the Douglas brothers to a lavish banquet held at Edinburgh Castle. The feast was promoted as a gesture of peace and reconciliation.

The brothers accepted the invitation and arrived at the banquet with their companion, Sir Malcolm Fleming of Cumbernauld (he was also serving as the guardian of the earl of Douglas). The banquet was lively. Tables were full of food. The men enjoyed roasted meats and silver goblets filled to the brim with wine. Musicians played soothing music, and laughter could be heard erupting across the hall. Even the young king, James II, was present, though it has never been confirmed whether he was made aware of the coup about to take place.

Eventually, the Douglas brothers noticed a shift in the mood. The music had stopped, and the laughter abruptly died. A man approached their table and slammed the head of a black bull on it. This was a traditional symbol of death.

Everything happened in an instant. The Douglas brothers did not have enough time to react. Crichton, taking advantage of their confusion, quickly ordered his men to seize the brothers. They were dragged from their table and brought outside. Some said that James II let out a protest, pleading with the chancellor to spare the guests. Yet, his pleas fell on deaf ears. Yes, he was king, but he was also a child. His words carried no weight among the power-hungry lords who surrounded him.

In the courtyard of the castle, the Douglas brothers were given a trial. This was only a performative act; their fates had already been sealed. They were executed right there and then, along with their guardian, Malcolm Fleming. Perhaps a faint smile could be seen on the faces of Crichton and Livingston as they watched the heads of their rivals roll. They had successfully done this terrible deed under the guise of royal justice.

Unsurprisingly, the violence did not stop there. The Douglas family soon retaliated, laying a siege on Edinburgh Castle. The murder also led to a significant shift of power in the Scottish court, throwing the nation into deeper political instability.

Interestingly, James II himself would get his own hands dirty years later. Some claimed that having witnessed the unfair murder of the Douglas brothers led James II to grow paranoid. He would later repeat a somewhat similar trap to eradicate his rival. But this time, instead of a lively feast, James invited another head of the Douglas family to a meeting at Stirling Castle with the promise of safe conduct. When the earl refused to comply with his order, the king lunged and stabbed him in the neck.

The Harrowing Murders By Burke and Hare

When Europe entered the Age of Enlightenment, Edinburgh enjoyed a period of change. The city had once been full of nearly endless battles and violent political feuds between medieval kings and nobles; now, the city was known as a center of learning. By the 1820s, Edinburgh's medical schools boomed. Students and physicians flocked to the city as it became the leading center, especially for anatomical studies.

Although this rising interest in human anatomy brought invaluable advancements to medicine and deepened our understanding of the human body, it also gave rise to a morbid dilemma. The law allowed students and medical professionals to perform dissections, but only on the bodies of executed criminals. In a time when executions greatly declined, these medical professionals saw a major decline in the supply of cadavers. To some, this was an opportunity for business, and these opportunists resorted to grave robbing.

Referred to as "resurrectionists," these body snatchers would embark on their mission late at night. They dug up fresh corpses and sold them to surgeons.

But then came two men who would take the shady business further. Much further.

Their names were William Burke and William Hare. Burke was an Irish immigrant and a former laborer. He first met Burke in 1827 when he moved into his lodging house. Their story began in November of the same year. An elderly lodger named Donald had recently died of natural causes. The old man had been ill for some time and owed Hare rent. Now that he was dead, Hare became worried about his financial loss. This was when his sinister mind hatched a plan. He turned to Burke and told him his idea of how to benefit from the death.

Instead of reporting the death of the old man, the two men decided to secretly sell the corpse to an anatomist at Edinburgh Medical College, Dr. Robert Knox. In return, they received a payment of seven pounds and ten shillings, an amount equivalent to nearly nine hundred pounds today. This was a considerable sum of money. It was comparable to more than two weeks' wages for a skilled worker.

The two men saw an opportunity worth repeating, but they had no time to wait for someone to fall ill and die of their sickness. They realized murder was the way to go.

They typically targeted the poor, the sick, the marginalized, and even the lonely. These were the people who would not be missed. Burke and Hare even came up with a method to carefully kill their victims in order to deliver their bodies in the most perfect condition. First, they lured their victims to their lodgings. Then, they would ply their victims with alcohol so that they were semi-conscious. Afterward, the two would compress their victim's chest while closing their mouth and nose. This suffocated their victims in mere seconds. This technique, later dubbed "Burking," left little to no visible marks on the corpse, making it perfect for anatomical dissection and unlikely to arouse suspicion.

In just a year, Burke and Hare managed to murder at least sixteen people, including a disabled boy and a local prostitute named Mary Paterson. When they delivered Paterson's body to Dr. Knox, her appearance surprised him. Her body appeared as if she had died only a few seconds ago. It's plausible that Dr. Knox was curious about the methods used by the two men, but he never asked them. It was strictly business; he paid and said his goodbye.

Their sinister business might have gone on for longer if not for a small mistake. The two lured and killed a woman named Margaret Docherty in November 1828. However, on that same night, they happened to host two lodgers, James and Ann Gray. They hid Margaret's body under a bed, but it was discovered by the two lodgers. The police were immediately alerted, which resulted in the arrest of the two men. However, proving they murdered anyone was difficult. Medical examiners failed to conclusively determine the cause of Margaret's death thanks to the method used by the two men. Without hard evidence, the case stalled.

A drawing of Burke murdering Margaret, with Hare watching.[17]

The authorities chose a different technique: break one of the men into confessing. They offered Hare immunity in exchange for testifying against Burke. Hare did not hesitate to betray his friend for the sake of his own life. He gave a detailed confession, including the methods they used to kill their victims. Burke was convicted and hanged before a crowd on January 28th, 1829. His body was then publicly dissected.

Hare was released as per the deal. What happened to him afterward remains a mystery. With his name despised by everyone, he vanished into obscurity. Some even suggested that he was blinded in an attack, although others claimed he fled the country. Dr. Knox also faced consequences. Although he was never prosecuted, his reputation was permanently tarnished.

It is safe to say that Burke's and Hare's crimes left a lasting impact. Their case led to the Anatomy Act of 1832, which expanded the legal supply of cadavers and finally ended the need for grave robbing and murderous shortcuts.

Chapter 7 – Anchors Aweigh

For many years, piracy has captured the imagination of many. Images of barrels of rum, chests full of plunder, and fluttering black flags come to mind. Not to mention the famous names like Blackbeard, Calico Jack, Anne Bonny, and the fictional Jack Sparrow. Piracy was all the rage during the late 1600s and early 1700s, a period often referred to as the Golden Age of Piracy. It was a period when British ports, such as Bristol and London, grew fat off sugar, slaves, and stolen Spanish gold. Even Queen Elizabeth herself subtly played a hand in such ventures; she knighted Francis Drake, despite his acts of outright theft and maritime violence.

A painting depicting a scene of a French ship under attack by pirates.[18]

Much of the world's attention on this age is fixated on the Caribbean and the blood-soaked waters off England's southern coast. However, few are aware that piracy was never just a Caribbean affair. Long before the

Spanish Main was plundered or the Jolly Roger struck terror on tropical tides, northern seas had already borne witness to their own age of raiders. Some might even say Scottish waters were seasoned with salt, blood, and the creak of oar-driven longships centuries before.

Scotland saw the arrival of its earliest pirate visitors, the Vikings, sometime around 795 CE. These Norsemen did not come in peace. They cut through the waters of the North Sea in their longships, setting their anchors near Scottish coastal villages and towns. They raided monasteries, sacked settlements, and plundered nearly everything, from silver to livestock. They took captives. For centuries, these sea raiders were a constant threat to the northern and western shores of Scotland. Their most popular attacks were the ones at Lindisfarne and Iona, where many monks witnessed their fury.

In the 12th century, Sweyn Asleifsson came to prominence. Born in Caithness to a noble Norse family, he left his mark on the Orkney Islands, which served as his base. He was known to have plundered the coasts of Britain. He did so with royal permission at times, but he mostly did so without. Sweyn was not only active in raiding; he was also involved in open battle, often switching sides between Norse earls and Scottish lords. He would support whoever paid him more. His stories and adventures are preserved in Icelandic chronicles, which painted him as the embodiment of a warrior pirate.

Years later, as the Viking threat waned, Scotland saw a shift in piracy. Some turned to piracy out of necessity. The MacNeils of Barra indulged in acts of raids and plunder to sustain their lives. This Highlands clan lived on a rather unforgiving island. The soil was too poor for cultivation, so they turned to the sea for survival. They fished, but this alone was not enough to keep the clan alive. Any ship passing their line of sight became a target. English, Spanish, French, and even fellow Scots were seen as fair game. With this plunder, they built homes and thrived.

Whether it was driven by necessity or greed, piracy was no light offense. The Scottish government, though often slow to act, tried to assert its authority. It hunted pirates, especially the ones whose names were known across the seas, bringing them to trials, which were often held in port towns. Judges heard testimonies from a range of witnesses, including surviving victims and crew members. Evidence could range from stolen goods to confessions under pressure. If convicted, the punishment was often hanging. Their bodies were left exposed as a warning to those still roaming the sea.

Believe it or not, not even kings were protected from pirates. In 1406, the future King James I of Scotland (not to be confused with the later James VI of Scotland, who became James I of England) was sent away by his father to France, who feared that the political strife in Scotland would endanger his heir. During this journey, twelve-year-old James was kidnapped by English pirates. His ship was robbed, and the pirates handed him over to King Henry IV of England. James, now a political hostage, remained in England for eighteen years.

William Kidd

Some may get confused with the differences between pirates and privateers, especially since both roamed the oceans with cannons and sought treasure. One of the few things that differentiated these two types of men was not their actions but whose name they sailed under. A pirate was an outlaw, plain and simple. They answered to no one and were condemned by everyone. Privateers, on the other hand, roamed the ocean with a government-issued permit known as a letter of marque and reprisal. This was basically a royal document that turned them into legal predators. If the captain of a ship were in possession of this paper, they could capture enemy vessels and plunder their goods without being charged with piracy. Their spoils, however, had to be shared with the ruler who had commissioned them.

One of the most prominent privateer-turned-pirates in Scotland was William Kidd. Born in Dundee sometime in 1654, Kidd always had a love for the sea. His life led him to become the captain of his own ship. In the late 1690s, he was backed by one of England's most powerful men, the earl of Bellomont, who was also the governor of New York and New England, leading to Kidd earning a commission to protect English shipping interests. Kidd was to set sail and hunt the pirates that had been wreaking havoc in the Indian Ocean.

He departed aboard the *Adventure Galley* in 1696. Trouble, however, brewed sooner than he expected. It took nearly a year just for him to reach the Indian Ocean. Most of his crew were former privateers themselves, so it was not surprising that they all expected plunder soon. When the voyage dragged on without success, morale plummeted. The crew grew restless and were on the verge of mutiny, especially when Kidd refused to attack ships that he believed did not fall under his commission. His gunner, William Moore, was very vocal. He argued with Kidd, accusing him of cowardice for refusing to attack Dutch ships. While Moore believed these ships had lucrative loot just waiting for them to plunder, Kidd argued they were illegal targets. The argument soon turned violent. Kidd reportedly struck Moore on the head with an iron-hooped bucket. Moore survived, but only for the night; he succumbed to his wound the next day.

Captain Kidd (in red) welcoming young women aboard his ship docked in New York Harbor.[19]

Things continued to unravel. Frustration and desperation mounted, and Kidd's actions grew increasingly aggressive. At times, he used French colors as a ruse to approach his targets; this was standard naval practice, though it was still risky. His most infamous act came in January 1698 when he captured the *Quedagh Merchant*, an Indian vessel filled with goods.

Kidd and his crew succeeded in capturing the four-hundred-ton treasure ship, which sailed with French papers. At first, this appeared to be a jackpot. The cargo was undeniably precious, filled with silk, muslin, calico, sugar, and other valuable trade goods. The situation, however, proved far more complex. Unbeknownst to Kidd, part of the cargo belonged to a powerful courtier serving the Mughal emperor.

This detail changed everything. The East India Company, anxious to preserve its fragile alliance with the Mughal Empire, feared that any perception of British attacks on Mughal interests could collapse its trade network. Seeking to protect itself, the East India Company branded Kidd a pirate. After abandoning and burning the captured ship near Madagascar, Kidd eventually sailed for the Atlantic, hoping to clear his name. In 1699, he traveled to Boston to plead his case before Lord

Bellomont, the very man who had once invested in his mission.

Unfortunately, news of his plunder had already preceded him, and there was growing pressure from Parliament and the East India Company to condemn his actions. Bellomont, now politically exposed and facing scrutiny from his Whig allies and Tory enemies, saw Kidd as a liability. Some historians suggest that Kidd was made into a scapegoat.

The trial in London was riddled with political tension. Documents that might have supported Kidd's legal case, particularly the French papers, were either lost or never presented. The public was thirsty for blood, and Parliament was eager to please the East India Company.

Captain William Kidd was found guilty. On May 23rd, 1701, he was hanged at Execution Dock in London. At first, the rope snapped, which many viewed as a bad omen. A second noose was wrapped around his neck, which held. His tarred body was left suspended in a gibbet over the River Thames. It was meant to serve as a warning and scare those who wished to go down the road of plunder.

The body of William Kidd displayed near Tilbury in Essex.[20]

Alexander Dalzeel

Of course, this warning did not terrify everyone, least of all a man like Alexander Dalzeel, though historians have long struggled to separate the man from the myth.

One legend says that Dalzeel, born around 1660, was familiar with the sea as a young boy. In 1685, when he arrived in Madagascar, Dalzeel was said to have crossed paths with the infamous pirate Captain Henry Every. He was soon enlisted into the captain's crew and played a role in the seizure of *Ganj-i-Sawai*. This Mughal treasure ship carried more than just treasure; aboard was also the Mughal emperor's daughter, who was on her way to an arranged marriage. Henry Every fell in love with the princess and handed Dalzeel the command of his own vessel and crew.

Years later, Dalzeel bade farewell to Every and sailed westward toward the Caribbean. Yet, fortune proved elusive. There were no targets, and slowly, his supplies dwindled. His crew was on the brink of starvation when, suddenly, they spotted a ship on the horizon. However, this was not the kind of target they had hoped for. It was a heavily armed Spanish war galleon. But this galleon was alone, which led Dalzeel to believe that it had been separated from its escorts.

Dalzeel made a daring decision. He steered his ship, which was much smaller compared to the galleon, closer to the target. The Spanish captain was informed of the approaching ship, yet he underestimated it. The captain retreated into his cabin and continued his game of cards.

Dalzeel was not planning on submitting to the odds. To ensure there would be no turning back, he was said to have ordered a hole drilled in the side of his vessel, leaving the crew with no choice but to fight or drown.

The fight was violent, and the Spanish were defeated. The captain was still at his table when Dalzeel's men boarded the galleon and stormed into his quarters with pistols drawn.

Dalzeel then sailed the galleon to Jamaica. Perhaps his confidence had been boosted by the previous success, as he aimed higher. He targeted a fleet of twelve Spanish ships accompanied by a man-of-war. His attempt to intercept the fleet failed terribly. Dalzeel and his crew were apprehended. Since they agreed to surrender rather than fight to the death, Dalzeel and his crew were spared from the usual punishment often subjected to pirates.

Still, Dalzeel showed no remorse for his actions. He returned to Jamaica later on and began outfitting another ship. But history would soon repeat itself. Off the coast of Cuba, his vessel was overtaken once more. This time around, he was captured by a squadron of three Spanish warships. He was sentenced to be hanged at sea.

Dalzeel refused to accept this end. As if luck was on his side, he managed to escape after stabbing a guard. Using two empty jugs as flotation devices, he drifted to shore, where he met a band of pirates. Here, he convinced the pirates to join his mission. He planned to capture the very warship that had imprisoned him. However, while nearing Jamaica, their stolen ship was struck by a sudden storm and sank. Dalzeel survived, this time in a canoe.

Whether all of these events happened exactly as described is hard to say. Much of Dalzeel's life comes from pirate lore and should be taken with a degree of caution. What is more historically verifiable are the events during the War of the Spanish Succession. Dalzeel sailed under a different flag. He captained the vessel *Agrippa* and was issued a commission as a privateer by the French Crown. Since he was a staunch Jacobite, Dalzeel sailed under the banner of the exiled James Stuart. He waged war on Britain and its allies, capturing merchant vessels and disrupting enemy trade routes. But his success was temporary. He was eventually captured and brought to England. Dalzeel was then tried in 1712 for treason and was sentenced to be hanged, drawn, and quartered.

Then came a twist. The earl of Mar interceded, and Dalzeel received a royal pardon. Freed once more, he made for French waters. Known for being dishonest, Dalzeel yet again betrayed his supposed benefactors. He seized a French ship near Le Havre and, in one of his more chilling acts, ordered the captured crew's necks to be tied to their heels and had them thrown overboard. Dalzeel was eventually captured in Scotland. He was extradited to London, where he was charged with piracy. He was finally hanged on December 15th, 1715.

John Gow

Born in 1698 in Wick, Caithness, John Gow's life began far from the warm waters of the Caribbean or the raiding routes of the Spanish Main. However, we know little of his early years. His family later relocated to Orkney. Some sources say his father was a prominent merchant. As a young man, Gow followed the tides, working as a sailor and later rising through the ranks in the merchant trade. However, in his late twenties, Gow deviated from the entrepreneurial path.

One of the few depictions of John Gow.[21]

Sometime in 1724, Gow was said to have been a part of a crew bound from London to Lisbon and back. For reasons lost to time, he tried to rally the men to mutiny. However, this plan was foiled before it could begin, as only a few chose to stand by his side. Even so, word of the attempt made its way through the London docks. With authorities likely closing in, Gow slipped away to Amsterdam. Here, he signed on as a second mate aboard the *Caroline*, a merchant ship heading to the Canary Islands. For months, the *Caroline* lingered in port at Santa Cruz on the island of La Palma, loading cargo—beeswax, leather, and fine woolens—for a voyage to Genoa, Italy. But while the hold filled, discontent festered above deck.

The atmosphere aboard the *Caroline* was tense. Rations had run short, and morale was incredibly low. The crew threw about complaints about their captain, Freneau. Some claimed he abused his authority and that he treated the men with contempt. Others voiced their discontent about how they had been cheated; they were sure they would never see their rightful pay. As time went on, disobedience crept into daily operations. Orders were met with silence or, worse, deliberate refusal.

Sensing that violence would soon erupt, Captain Freneau and his mate hid a stash of small arms in the cabin, which they would use should a fight break out. But unbeknownst to Freneau, two conspirators had overheard their conversation. To make matters worse for the captain, the man he tasked with readying the arms in the event of an uprising was none other than John Gow himself. He had no idea that Gow would be the very architect of the rebellion.

The moment arrived on the night of November 3rd, 1724. Everything seemed normal at first. Half the crew had retired below deck following evening prayers. Suddenly, there was a commotion. Someone shouted that a man had fallen overboard, prompting Freneau to rush to the rail. As he leaned over the side, Gow made his move. He stabbed the captain in the neck and fired two rounds into his stomach. The captain staggered backward, and the other mutineers hauled him overboard.

This was not yet the end of Freneau. The captain managed to hold on to a rope trailing the hull. He would not live for long, though. The mutineers soon discovered him, and they immediately cut the line. Freneau plunged into the sea, vanishing into the deep, black waters.

John Gow, now captain of the ship, gave the crew a choice. They could go back to their positions or accept the same fate as Freneau. Unsurprisingly, none chose death. And so, the *Caroline* was no more; it was reborn as the *Revenge.*

What followed was a brief but furious campaign of piracy off the Iberian coast. Gow's first known attack came on November 12th, targeting a British vessel called the *Delight.* Nine days later, he seized another named the *Sarah.* These British sailors were usually set adrift, saved for those Gow deemed valuable and skilled. Those men were offered a place aboard his ship. However, the more influence Gow gained, the more closely he came under the authorities' watchful eye.

When supplies began to run low, Gow made the decision to return home. To ensure safe sailing, the flags were changed, and the *Revenge* was renamed the *George.* Gow disguised himself as a wealthy trader who went by the name Smith. For a while, this worked. Gow mingled with the gentry, courted a local heiress named Miss Gordon, and dined with merchants and landowners.

Things changed for the worse when a passing trader caught a glimpse of the wealthy Mr. Smith. Some accounts suggested that the trader was once a prisoner aboard the *Revenge,* who had either escaped or been released. He recognized Gow's face and warned the authorities. John Gow had been unmasked.

However, Gow refused to go down the path of submission. Instead, he doubled down. On February 10th, 1725, he and his men staged a raid on the Hall of Clestrain, a prominent estate on Orkney. It was successful, but this victory was fleeting. Flushed from his triumph, Gow led his crew in an attempt to attack yet another remote mansion. This time, the sea itself betrayed him. His ship ran aground on the Calf of Eday. Stranded and surrounded, the crew finally surrendered. John Gow was taken to London, where he stood trial at the Old Bailey. He was found guilty of piracy and sentenced to death.

Helen Gloag

This particular story was not of a marauder but of a Scottish woman whose life offers a different lens on the far-reaching consequences of piracy. Helen Gloag was born in 1750. Although she grew up in modest surroundings—her father was a blacksmith—Helen was meant to have a destiny that no one could ever predict. It all began when she set out to find a better life beyond the rugged hills of Scotland. At the ripe age of nineteen, she boarded a ship bound for the Americas. However, Helen never arrived at her destination.

Somewhere off the coast of Spain, her ship was intercepted by Barbary corsairs. These pirates prowled the waters of the Mediterranean and Atlantic. They were typically sanctioned by the sultan of Morocco and other North African rulers. More often than not, these Barbary pirates made their fortune capturing European vessels and selling their passengers and crew at auction. Helen was among the unlucky ones. She was brought to a Moroccan slave market. Helen was confident that her life was over and that she would never taste freedom again.

Her thoughts were proved wrong when the slave market was visited by Sidi Mohammed bin Abdallah, the sultan of Morocco himself. Helen, with her shimmering green eyes and burning red hair, caught the sultan's attention. He was immediately captured by her beauty, and she was taken into his harem. To the surprise of the Moroccan courtiers, this foreign woman, who had no noble blood running through her veins, quickly rose through the ranks. She soon became the sultan's favored consort. Some sources even claim she was made the sultan's fourth wife. In time, she came to be known by a new name among the court: the Empress of Morocco.

Helen was not a passive woman; she was said to have wielded quiet influence. Although the exact extent of her power remains debated, it is widely believed that she interceded on behalf of European captives, persuading the sultan to release several Christian slaves. This was a bold and unlikely feat for a foreign woman in a royal Muslim court. Letters and accounts from passing diplomats described her presence at the palace and whispered of the strange tale of the Scottish girl who ruled in silks and sandalwood.

Of course, power, especially gained by accident or by beauty, did not often last long. When the sultan died in 1790, the succession crisis that followed turned deadly. His son, Yazid, seized the throne violently. Suspicious of anyone connected to his father's regime, especially foreigners, Yazid ordered the execution of Helen's two sons and possibly Helen herself.

Chapter 8 – Burning at the Stake

The sea has always been unrelenting. It can appear calm one second and totally chaotic the next. Anne of Denmark was one of the many who tasted the wrath of the sea, along with King James VI of Scotland.

Anne left the comfort of her homeland in September 1589. She was supposed to set sail to Scotland, where she would finally unite with her husband, King James (the two had been married by proxy a month prior). Their union was extremely important. Scotland was largely Protestant under James. Denmark was a powerful Protestant nation under King Frederick II. Their union could cement a Protestant alliance and counterbalance the Catholic powers of Spain and France in Europe. Plus, James VI was the son of Mary, Queen of Scots, whose life was shrouded in controversy. His marriage to a princess of noble blood could help him strengthen his legitimacy as king and set the stage for a stable royal lineage.

However, misfortune soon struck Anne's fleet. A great storm battered the Danish fleet, forcing them to halt the voyage and seek refuge in the Norwegian port of Oslo. When the news of his wife's troubles reached him, King James made preparations to set sail to Norway, hoping he could escort his wife to Scotland himself. They were eventually united in Oslo and married in person in November of the same year. However, their return journey went south. It was as if the universe did not agree with their union, as the Scottish fleet faced the wrath of the North Sea. Waves thrashed violently, and lightning split the sky. The merciless storm made James and Anne turn back for shelter in Norway.

To modern eyes, this episode was nothing more than just the work of Mother Nature. To James, however, the misfortune felt like an omen. He started to suspect that the storm was conjured by those who wished to see him dead.

His suspicions grew more when he heard troubling news at the Danish court. Several women had been arrested and accused of witchcraft. It was said they were the ones responsible for raising the disasters that had battered Anne's ship. Known as the Copenhagen witch trials, this was the first major witch trial in Denmark. The first to have been interrogated was Anna Koldings. After enduring torture, she confessed. She mentioned the names of five other women and revealed they were capable of summoning demons. These demons had been ordered to crawl up the keel of Anne's ship and rock it with unnatural storms. The tale shocked many. The women were burned at the stake at Kronborg Castle.

The seeds of paranoia had been sown. King James was convinced that his life was in danger; if witches had conspired to kill his bride, what would stop them from trying the same with him? When he finally returned to Scotland in 1590, the king brought with him not only a wife but an obsession. He wanted to cleanse his nation of dark forces and sorcery, and he would soon authorize trials, brutal torture, and executions in his pursuit of witches. He even went so far as to write books on demonology.

The Maid Accused of Using Magic

Geillis Duncan was not born into wealth. She was only a teenager from the small town of Tranent (located in East Lothian) when she became a maid. She worked under David Seton, a bailie (a position similar to that of a magistrate). Seton was known to be a strict Protestant. He was a strong believer in religious order and moral righteousness, so it was not surprising that he expected those under his roof to do the same. As a maid, Geillis was nearly invisible to her master, but over time, her strange behavior began to attract Seton's attention.

Every other night, Geillis would wait for everyone to fall asleep and leave the house. It was strange for such a young woman at that time to embark on late-night excursions. She would return before dusk. Eventually, Seton heard whispers of Geillis's abilities to cure the sick. This undoubtedly raised his suspicions. After all, Geillis had no medical training, and he had never heard her pray. Seton was certain that his maid was up to no good; perhaps she was out at night meeting the devil himself.

And so, he went to confront her. He was probably expecting a tearful confession where Geillis begged for mercy, but Geillis stood firm and insisted that she had done nothing wrong. Seton viewed her denial as proof of guilt. With his influence in the Scottish government, Seton was free to conduct his own investigations.

Geillis was arrested, interrogated, and subjected to various forms of torture. First, Seton used the pilliwinks on her. This was a type of thumbscrew device made of iron. He clamped the device around her fingers and demanded answers from her. When she did not give the answer he desired, he slowly tightened the device until her nails cracked and the flesh beneath was crushed. Still, Geillis did not confess, which led Seton to intensify his cruelty.

Thumbscrews or pilliwinks were typically used in torture chambers.[22]

Geillis was then stripped of her clothing. Every strand of her body hair was shaved, from her head to both of her arms and even her pubic region. This humiliating act was done to prepare her for the "inspection." Considered a standard procedure in a witch trial, every single part of her body was examined. Seton was looking for what they called the devil's mark. A unique blemish or mole on a person's skin, including birthmarks, was seen as a sign of their involvement with the devil. They believed these marks were the result of the devil suckling the skin of his servant. Modern scholars have not hesitated to call this what it was—ritualized sexual violence sanctioned by law and religion.

Geillis's inspection went on for quite a while until Seton eventually declared that he had found a mark on her throat. We can never be sure what exactly the mark was; it could have been a mole or perhaps a slight discoloration on her skin. Whatever it was, Geillis was a step closer to death.

A painting depicting the examination of a witch.[33]

The pilliwinks were not the only torture device used to extract confessions from accused witches. Another inhumane instrument used across Scotland and other European nations was the breast ripper. Its iron claws were sharp enough to easily pierce and tear flesh. Often, the device would be heated in the fire before being applied to the breasts of the accused.

Another form of this device was known as the iron spider. Similar in function, this particular device was fixed to the wall. The breasts of the accused were then fixed to the claws of the device before their bodies were pulled away by their torturers, thus ripping their breasts off. Although there was no record of Geillis going through this unspeakable torture, such tools were usually present in interrogation chambers.

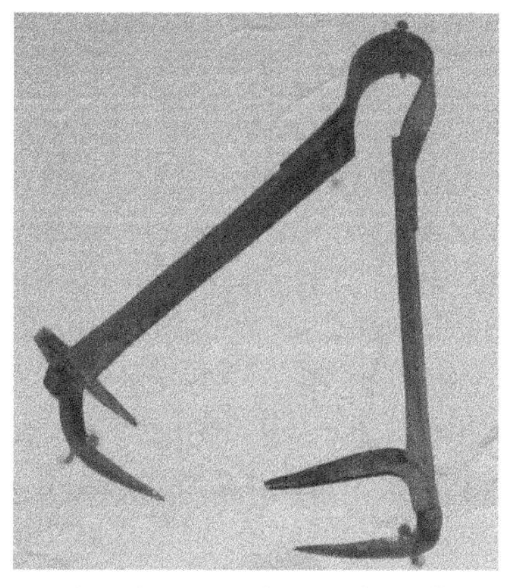

A 15th-century breast ripper.[34]

There was also the scold's bridle, a spiked iron muzzle designed to be fastened around the head. The device was fitted with four sharp prongs. One would press into the cheeks of the accused, and the other two pressed into their tongue. It was designed to silence the victims. Those who had the device on for too long could choke on their own blood. The device was initially created for husbands to punish and silence their wives, especially those who were thought to have spoken too freely and often nagged at their husbands. However, it was also commonly used during witch trials.

A woman wearing a scold's bridle.[25]

When it came to signs of witchcraft, the authorities looked for more than a birthmark or a mole. Red hair was considered a damning trait. More often than not, the bright, fiery color was linked to seduction, unruliness, and bad luck. Red hair is genetically rare; even today, it is estimated that less than 2 percent of the world's population has it. While modern societies may view red hair as a symbol of beauty, people back then thought otherwise. Standing out was not always a blessing.

If a person, especially a woman, happened to be left-handed, they risked being named a witch. The left side of the body had long been associated with darkness and evil in many cultures. Believe it or not, the Latin word for "left" is *sinistra*, which is the root of the English word "sinister." It is safe to say that the witch trials were a time when the body became a map of guilt.

As for Geillis Duncan, she eventually broke. Whether it was the unimaginable pain caused by the pilliwinks or the psychological torment of isolation and the physical violation under the guise of examination, Geillis gave in and confessed. Like many other women in her shoes, Geillis delivered a detailed, fantastical story. These tales were then spread across Scotland, inviting terror and feeding the already growing paranoia that witches lurked in every village, plotting the downfall of anyone they despised.

Geillis claimed that she did not work alone. According to her confession, she participated in secret gatherings held in North Berwick and Edinburgh. This was where witches—both men and women—would convene to perform dark rituals. It was said that Satan himself appeared before them, dressed in all black. Their main topic of discussion remained the same throughout all of the gatherings. According to Geillis, Satan had instructed them to rid the world of King James VI of Scotland. To seal their obedience, the witches allegedly kissed the devil's bare buttocks to mark their pact.

Drawing on a pamphlet, depicting witches' meeting with the devil.[36]

Geillis even went so far as to describe the methods and rituals the witches performed to bring misfortune upon the king and his bride. The first step involved the witches digging up corpses from local graveyards. They would then dismember the dead before tying the rotten severed limbs to the bodies of cats. While cats were highly revered in parts of the world like ancient Egypt, the Western world viewed the creature with suspicion. Cats were thought to indicate the presence of evil. It could be the devil himself or perhaps a witch in disguise.

The next step of the ritual required the witches to throw the limbs into the sea. Because of their actions, a wild storm was conjured. It was strong enough to sink ships and drown the most powerful kings and heroes. Geillis claimed this was how they nearly killed James during his voyage.

These stories tapped directly into King James's deepest fears. Until this moment, he had only suspicions. But this confession confirmed it all. King James decided to take a direct role in the trials. He was present in the interrogations and, at times, even questioned the accused himself. This was the beginning of the North Berwick witch trials.

People accused of witchcraft brought before King James.[27]

Interestingly, Geillis also exposed the names of others believed to have indulged in witchcraft. The list included Agnes Sampson, a respected healer and midwife; Doctor John Fian, a schoolmaster; a noblewoman named Barbara Napier; and Euphame MacCalzean, who was the daughter of a judge. These people were far from mere commoners. They were known for their wisdom, healing skills, and social standing. Ironically, these were the things that made them targets.

According to Geillis Duncan, Agnes Sampson was the eldest witch. In reality, she was an elderly woman, known among the villagers as a comforting midwife. She was described as a wise woman, as she was capable of treating the sick. Perhaps she was too wise for her time. Agnes was captured after Geillis mentioned her name. She was imprisoned in the dungeons of Holyrood Palace, where each day she had to go through the same gruesome torture and interrogations that befell Geillis and others.

Similar to Geillis, Agnes held firm. She denied every charge at first. She was eventually brought before James VI and a council of nobles. Yet Agnes refused to confess, claiming she was only a humble healer who used herbs and prayers rather than demonic chants and rituals. Still, no one believed her; her refusal to confess was met with cruelty.

Agnes was then subjected to the examination. She was stripped naked and shaved from head to toe for the authorities to search for the devil's mark. After claiming they found the mark on her private part, Agnes was forced to wear the scold's bridle for days. On the days when she did not wear the scold's bridle, Agnes had a cord or a rope tied around her head. The torturers would twist it tightly, often causing bleeding or unconsciousness. Agnes was also deprived of sleep.

The torment eventually broke her resistance. Agnes chose to confess to all fifty-three indictments against her. This was what the authorities had been waiting for. She was sentenced to death on January 28th, 1591. She was first garroted (a method of strangulation). Once her soul left the world, her body was burned at the stake on Castlehill.

Dr. John Fian (also known as John Cunninghame) also faced a harrowing fate after his arrest. He was well educated. As a schoolmaster and scholar in Prestonpans, Fian, he knew Latin and was well versed in theology. Like Agnes and Geillis, he denied all charges initially until the authorities broke his spirit.

John was subjected to the pilliwinks and the boot. The latter was a brutal contraption capable of splintering the bones of the lower legs by driving wedges between the foot and a wooden casing. John still refused to confess even after he was threatened with being racked. However, no one could withstand the continuous brutality. In the end, he confessed to making a pact with the devil. He even said he had renounced Christianity and led a coven of witches.

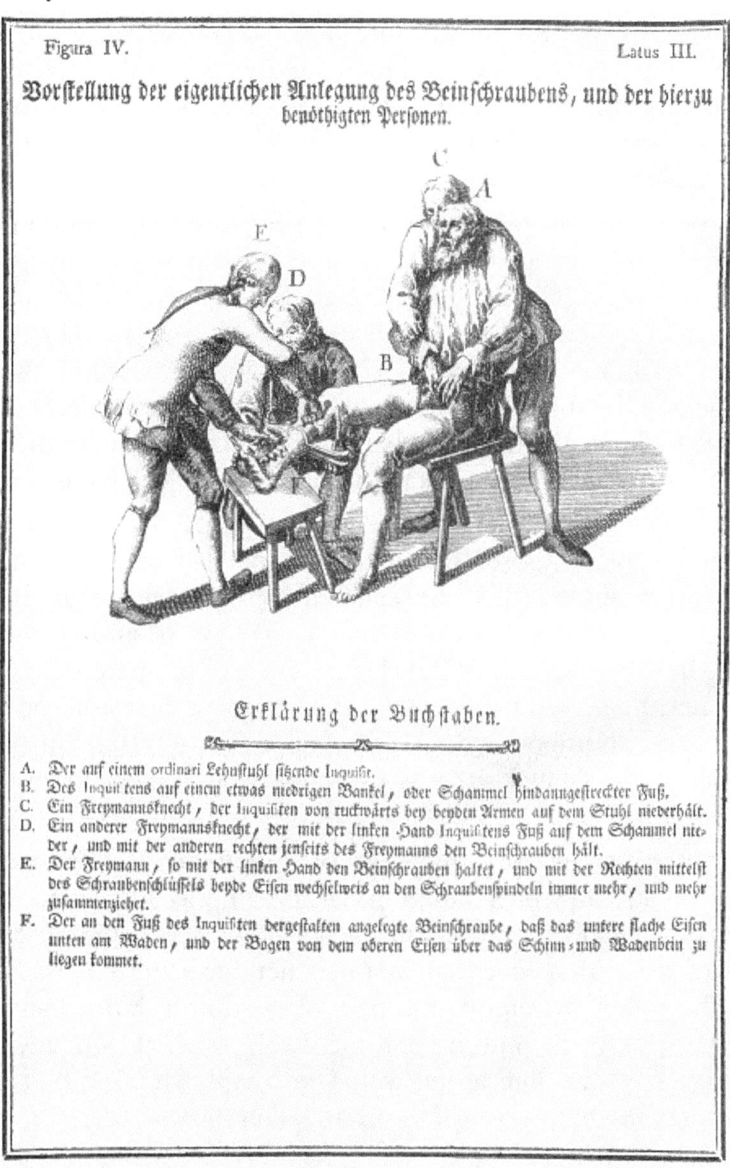

A man going through the boot, also known as leg screwing.[38]

Interestingly, Dr. Fian also testified against Francis Stewart, the 5th Earl of Bothwell and King James's own cousin, who held significant influence in court. According to John's claim, Bothwell played a hand in attempting to kill the king. He was said to have consorted with witches and approved of them using magic to eradicate the king.

The accusation was not a surprise to James VI. The king had long held suspicions about his cousin. He believed that Bothwell was harboring ambitions for the throne. The alleged claim was a perfect opportunity for James to remove him from the court without anyone else interrupting. Bothwell was arrested for treason. He managed to escape from prison and fled into exile. However, he never succeeded in recovering his reputation.

Barbara Napier also experienced a terrible downfall. Coming from a noble family and having ties to the royal court (she was a lady-in-waiting to Lady Jean Lyon, Countess of Angus), her capture in May 1591 was quite a surprise. The evidence against her was flimsy, yet the authorities pursued her case aggressively. Her biggest accusation was her involvement in the mysterious death of the earl of Angus in August 1588. According to Geillis Duncan, Barbara's residence in Edinburgh was one of the places where witches gathered to discuss their evil plans. It did not help that Barbara was a friend of Francis Stewart.

Barbara Napier was sentenced to be strangled and burned at the stake. Sources suggest that she claimed to be pregnant at the time, perhaps hoping the authorities would cancel or postpone her death sentence. In order to confirm the claim, James VI ordered a physician to examine her. If she was lying about the pregnancy, she was to be burned and publicly disemboweled. What happened to Barbara remains uncertain. Some claimed she was executed, while others suggested that she was imprisoned until 1592.

Even more tragic was the case of Euphame MacCalzean. The daughter of an influential judge, MacCalzean was known to be well educated and highly respected by those in the legal sphere. She was accused of using dark magic to bewitch her husband and was said to possess the power to remove the pain of childbirth. Since pain during labor was seen as a punishment for Eve's original sin, any act of suppressing it meant interfering with God's will. Her compassion was viewed as a crime in the eyes of the church and the courts.

The MacCalzean family feud also added weight to her unfair downfall. She had argued with her uncle over a land dispute in Cliftonhall in Kirkliston. The issue was said to have resulted in MacCalzean killing his son—her own cousin—through the use of sorcery. She was also reported to have attended a gathering of witches at Acheson's Haven, where witches handed the image of King James to the devil, an act believed to symbolize their desire to murder him. Not given a chance to defend herself from the accusations, MacCalzean was tied to a stake and burned alive. Her wealth and properties were seized by King James VI. He then gave them to his favorites. Her estate of Cliftonhall was handed to Sir James Sandilands of Slamannan, and her house on Edinburgh's High Street was gifted to an officer in the royal stables known as John Shaw.

As for Geillis Duncan, the one who mentioned the names of these people and the one who went through grueling torture, she found herself tied to a stake on the slopes of Edinburgh's Castlehill on December 4th, 1591. She was not alone. Beside her was another condemned woman named Bessie Thomson.

As the pyres crackled and smoke began to fill the air, the two women retracted their confessions and attempted to cleanse the names of those they had mentioned. However, their pleas were ignored. The fire consumed their bodies.

The fear of witches and magic did not stop after the end of the North Berwick witch trials. People continued to accuse others of witchcraft for nearly a century and a half. Between the 16th and 17th centuries, at least four thousand people were accused of making pacts with the devil and using magic to harm others. The vast majority of them were women. The rate of executions in Scotland was five times the European average, making Scotland's witch hunts among the most ferocious.

The witch panic greatly intensified during times of political upheaval or religious fervor. At times, royal commissions were established to seek out and prosecute suspected witches. England, in particular, had its own witchfinder named Matthew Hopkins. He claimed to have held the office of Witchfinder General, though the title was never officially approved by Parliament.

It was only in the mid-1600s that skepticism began to take over. Judges and scholars questioned the validity of witchcraft evidence, especially when it was clear that confessions were the result of coercion.

As time went on, the use of torture, once defended as a righteous tool, began to lose moral and legal standing.

One of the last witch cases was that of Janet Horne. Originating from Dornoch in the Scottish Highlands, Horne was arrested for witchcraft in 1727. One of the most peculiar accusations laid onto her was that she possessed the power to transform her daughter into a pony. Witnesses claimed to have seen Horne riding her daughter to meet the devil. Her neighbors also spoke of her strange behavior and her wandering mind. Scholars today believe that she might have suffered from dementia, which was greatly misunderstood at that time.

Horne was subjected to terror. She was stripped, tarred, and paraded through town in a barrel. After these episodes of torture and humiliation, she was burned alive. Her daughter, who was also accused of witchcraft, managed to escape execution.

Janet Horne was the last person to be executed for witchcraft in Scotland. In 1735, Parliament passed the Witchcraft Act, formally repealing the crime of witchcraft. From then on, belief in magic or sorcery was no longer punishable by death, though some communities continued to hold their own superstitions and judgments for years to come. In 2022, the Scottish government took a symbolic step. It issued an official apology and acknowledged that these trials and executions were a national injustice. Although it was too late—many had suffered and died without having a chance to prove their innocence—at least the names of those who had been accused were cleansed at last.

Conclusion

It is worth noting that the story of Scotland is not only one of battles and kings but also of its people and their loyalties, superstitions, wounds, and their will to endure. The clan system, for instance, was not just a social structure but also a way of life. Ties of kinship ran deep, though they also paved the way to many feuds and fragile alliances that could be broken in a single night.

The people of Scotland cannot forget their past even if they wanted to, for even their land seems to retain memory. True, the castles that once housed monarchs now lie in crumbling silence, but they have become living museums, full of stories and remnants of grief, guilt, and even unfinished tales. The supernatural has always coexisted with Scottish history. Belief in omens, ghosts, and curses persisted through centuries of change. It became embedded in their daily lives as much as in lore. Whether truth or tale, these stories reflect a people deeply connected to the land and spirits.

The sea also played its part, giving way to more stories. Piracy was not limited only to the English coasts and the Caribbean. From the earliest Norse incursions to the age of privateers, piracy found fertile ground in Scotland's coves and islands. Here, the line between outlaw and hero was often blurry. Many who sailed under false flags returned home with gold in their pockets and enemies at their heels. While some found fame, their names known across the land and beyond, others ended up with a noose wrapped tightly around their neck.

Even religion and belief could not always provide sanctuary for the Scots. There were times when a certain belief became the very instrument of persecution. Witchcraft, for instance, was a topic of terror, especially in the 16th and 17th centuries. This was a time when accusations ran rampant, turning neighbors or even families against each other. Those who were different, defiant, or simply unlucky were dragged before courts and tortured into confession. Of course, it was not just superstition that fueled these fires; fear, power, and the need for control in a world that was changing too quickly also played a role.

The history of Scotland is not written in a straight line. The land has had its own ups and downs, victories and tragedies. Scotland's stories are often rough, emotional, and full of layers, just like its rugged landscape.

Here's another book by Matt Clayton that you might like

Free Bonus from Captivating History (Available for a Limited time)

Hi History Lovers!

Now you have a chance to join our exclusive history list so you can get your first history ebook for free as well as discounts and a potential to get more history books for free!

Simply visit the link below to join.

Or, Scan the QR code!

captivatinghistory.com/ebook

Also, make sure to follow us on Facebook, X, and YouTube by searching for Captivating History.

Bibliography

"14 Haunted Castles in Scotland." (n.d.). Visit Scotland. Retrieved July 23, 2025, from https://www.visitscotland.com/things-to-do/attractions/castles/haunted

"AD84 – Battle of Mons Graupius." (n.d.). Scotclans. Retrieved July 12, 2025, from https://www.scotclans.com/pages/ad84-battle-of-mons-graupius

Adkins, Laura. "The English Solomon – The Life of King James I." *Talking About History With Laura*, April 13, 2019. https://fortheloveofhistory.home.blog/2019/04/13/the-english-solomon-the-life-of-king-james-i/

"Anne of Denmark." (n.d.). Undiscovered Scotland. Retrieved July 27, 2025, from https://www.undiscoveredscotland.co.uk/usbiography/a/anneofdenmark.html

"Assassination of James I, King of Scots (1437)." (n.d.). Unofficial Royalty. Retrieved July 26, 2025, from https://www.unofficialroyalty.com/assassination-of-james-i-king-of-scots-1437/

Babas, Loubna. "Helen Gloag, Captured by Corsairs to Become Morocco's Scottish Empress." *Yabiladi*, October 27, 2017. https://en.yabiladi.com/articles/details/58786/helen-gloag-captured-corsairs-become.html

"Barbara Napier, Witch." *Engole*, December 3, 2018. https://engole.info/barbara-napier-witch/

Brown, Rebecca. "From Tudor to Stuart: When James I Arrived in England." *RSB*, March 25, 2018. https://rebeccastarrbrown.com/2018/03/25/the-accession-of-james-i/

Campsie, Alison. "The Story of Finella Who Killed a Scots King." *The Scotsman*, October 23, 2015. https://www.scotsman.com/arts-and-culture/the-story-of-finella-who-killed-a-scots-king-1491784

Cavendish, Richard. "Execution of Captain Kidd." *History Today*, May 5, 2001. https://www.historytoday.com/archive/months-past/execution-captain-kidd

Chakra, H. "The 10 Gruesome Steps of the William Wallace Death." *About History*, November 21, 2024. https://about-history.com/william-wallace-death/

Connolly, Susan B. "Mary and Isabella – The Women in Cages." *History...The Interesting Bits!*, December 8, 2018. https://historytheinterestingbits.com/tag/isabella-buchan/

"Experts Unearth Ancient Murder Victim in East Lothian." *BBC*, February 21, 2014. https://www.bbc.com/news/uk-scotland-edinburgh-east-fife-26287895

Farell, S. "Cats, Symbolism and the 16th Century Witch Craze." *Cheshire & Wain*, October 20, 2024. https://www.cheshireandwain.com/blogs/journal/cats-and-the-16th-century-witch-craze

Flantzer, Susan. "Sybilla of Normandy, Queen of Scots, Illegitimate Daughter of King Henry I of England." *Unofficial Royalty*, February 16, 2024. https://www.unofficialroyalty.com/sybilla-of-normandy-queen-of-scots-illegitimate-daughter-of-king-henry-i-of-england/

"Forgotten Scottish Pirates: Tales of Treachery and Treasure." (n.d.). History. Retrieved July 21, 2025, from https://www.history.co.uk/articles/the-forgotten-pirates-of-scotland

Hernandez, J. A. "Haunting of Ackergill Tower in Scotland." *J.A. Hernandez*, August 8, 2023. https://www.jahernandez.com/posts/haunting-of-ackergill-tower-in-scotland

Hislop, K. "Green Ladies of Crathes Castle." *Local Legends: Folklore, Culture & You*. (n.d.). Retrieved July 23, 2025, from https://localfolklore.weebly.com/green-ladies-of-crathes-castle.html

"James VI & I and the 'Unite' Coin." (n.d.). National Galleries Scotland. Retrieved July 26, 2025, from https://www.nationalgalleries.org/art-and-artists/features/king-james-vi-i---art-culture-jacobean-court/james-VI-I-and-the-unite-coin

Kate. "Hermitage Castle: A Hauntingly Beautiful Ruin in the Scottish Borders." *Scotland Itinerary Planning*, September 17, 2023. https://scotlanditineraryplanning.com/hermitage-castle/

Kingshill, Stewart, and Jennifer Westwood. *The Lore of Scotland: A Guide to Scottish Legends*. 2009. https://openlibrary.org/books/OL25081911M/The_lore_of_Scotland

"Lady Finella." (n.d.). Undiscovered Scotland. Retrieved July 16, 2025, from https://www.undiscoveredscotland.co.uk/usbiography/f/finella.html

"MacNab Clan History." (n.d.). Scotclans. Retrieved July 13, 2025, from https://www.scotclans.com/blogs/tu3/macnab-clan-history

Mclean, Dave. "The Tragic Tale of 16th Century Tranent Maid Geillis Duncan Who Inspired *Outlander* Witch." *The Scotsman*, September 26, 2019. https://www.scotsman.com/heritage-and-retro/heritage/the-tragic-tale-of-16th-century-tranent-maid-geillis-duncan-who-inspired-outlander-witch-637529

"Medieval Murder Uncovered in Scotland." (n.d.). *Medievalists.net*. Retrieved July 21, 2025, from https://www.medievalists.net/2014/02/medieval-murder-uncovered-scotland/

Milligan, Mark. "The Black Dinner: An Event That Inspired the 'Red Wedding' in *Game of Thrones*." *Heritage Daily*, June 20, 2021. https://www.heritagedaily.com/2021/06/the-black-dinner-an-event-that-inspired-the-red-wedding-in-game-of-thrones/139523

Porath, Jason. "Anne Farquharson-Mackintosh." *Rejected Princesses*. (n.d.). Retrieved July 16, 2025, from https://www.rejectedprincesses.com/princesses/anne-farquharson-mackintosh

Roberts, Adam. "They Make a Loneliness and They Call It Peace." *Adam's Notebook*, June 5, 2021. https://medium.com/adams-notebook/they-make-a-loneliness-and-they-call-it-peace-3a45125159ae

"Rout of Moy." (n.d.). Strathdearn. Retrieved July 15, 2025, from https://strathdearn.org/the-rout-of-moy/

"The Horrifying Execution of William Wallace." *Mercat Tours*, August 14, 2024. https://www.mercattours.com/blog-post/the-horrifying-execution-of-william-wallace

Tiwari, V. "Have You Heard of the First Scot to Be Recorded in History?" *STV News*, January 6, 2024. https://news.stv.tv/scotland/have-you-heard-of-calgacus-first-scot-recorded-in-history

Vallar, Cindy. "Scottish Pirates." *Pirates and Privateers*, October 7, 2005. http://www.cindyvallar.com/scottish.html

Watson, Callum. "How to Get Away With Murder (in Late Medieval Scotland): The Killing of John Comyn Revisited." *Knight of the Two Ls*, July 8, 2019. https://drcallumwatson.blogspot.com/2019/07/how-to-get-away-with-murder-in-late.html

Whelan, Ed. "Medieval Murder Victim in Scotland May Have Been a Pictish Royal." *Ancient Origins*, July 26, 2019. https://www.ancient-origins.net/news-history-archaeology/pict-0012353

Image Sources

1   https://commons.wikimedia.org/wiki/File:William_Wallace_Statue_,_
    Aberdeen2.jpg

2   Steve F-E-Cameron (Merlin-UK), CC BY-SA 3.0
    <https://creativecommons.org/licenses/by-sa/3.0>, via Wikimedia Commons:
    https://commons.wikimedia.org/wiki/File:S_F-E-
    CAMERON_LONDON_WALLACE_MEMORIAL_STBARTS.JPG

3   https://commons.wikimedia.org/wiki/File:Calgacus.JPG

4   William Hole, CC BY-SA 3.0 <https://creativecommons.org/licenses/by-sa/3.0>, via
    Wikimedia Commons: https://commons.wikimedia.org/wiki/File:
    War_of_Independence_figures_by_Wm_Hole.JPG

5   Otter, CC BY-SA 3.0 <http://creativecommons.org/licenses/by-sa/3.0/>, via
    Wikimedia Commons: https://commons.wikimedia.org/wiki/File:
    St_Bride%27s_Church_Douglas_-_The_Good_Sir_James.jpg

6   https://commons.wikimedia.org/wiki/File:Black_Agnes,_from_a_
    children%27s_history_book.jpg

7   Phillip Capper from Wellington, New Zealand, CC BY 2.0
    <https://creativecommons.org/licenses/by/2.0>, via Wikimedia Commons,
    https://commons.wikimedia.org/wiki/File:Dunbar_Harbour_and_Castle,_1987.jpg

8   Kim Traynor, CC BY-SA 3.0 <https://creativecommons.org/licenses/by-sa/3.0>, via
    Wikimedia Commons: https://commons.wikimedia.org/wiki/File:Robert_The_
    Bruce_Crowned_King_of_Scots.jpg

9   https://commons.wikimedia.org/wiki/File:Jacobite_broadside_-
    _Lady_Mackintosh_03.jpg

10 https://commons.wikimedia.org/wiki/File:JamesIEngland.jpg

11 https://commons.wikimedia.org/wiki/File:James_I_de_Critz_Mirror_of_GB_(cropped).jpg

12 Kim Traynor, CC BY-SA 3.0 <https://creativecommons.org/licenses/by-sa/3.0>, via Wikimedia Commons: https://commons.wikimedia.org/wiki/File:Edinburgh_Castle_from_the_North.JPG

13 Lucas Kendall / Crathes Castle 2025: https://commons.wikimedia.org/wiki/File:Crathes_Castle_2025.jpg

14 Postdlf, CC BY-SA 3.0 <http://creativecommons.org/licenses/by-sa/3.0/>, via Wikimedia Commons: https://commons.wikimedia.org/wiki/File:Hermitage_Castle_06.jpg

15 https://commons.wikimedia.org/wiki/File:Ackergill.JPG

16 Phouka at English Wikipedia, CC BY-SA 3.0 <http://creativecommons.org/licenses/by-sa/3.0/>, via Wikimedia Commons: https://commons.wikimedia.org/wiki/File:Scotland.Sanquhar01.jpg

17 https://commons.wikimedia.org/wiki/File:Burke_Murdering_Margery_Campbell.jpg

18 https://commons.wikimedia.org/wiki/File:A_French_Ship_and_Barbary_Pirates_(c_1615)_by_Aert_Anthoniszoon.jpg

19 https://commons.wikimedia.org/wiki/File:Captain_Kidd_in_New_York_Harbor_cph.3f06373.jpg

20 https://commons.wikimedia.org/wiki/File:Hanging_of_William_Kidd.jpg

21 Geo. S. Harris and Sons, CC0, via Wikimedia Commons: https://commons.wikimedia.org/wiki/File:John_Gow,_Execution_of_Gow,_from_the_Pirates_of_the_Spanish_Main_series_(N19)_for_Allen_%26_Ginter_Cigarettes_MET_DP835023.jpg

22 Anagoria, CC BY 3.0 <https://creativecommons.org/licenses/by/3.0>, via Wikimedia Commons: https://commons.wikimedia.org/wiki/File:16XX_Thumbscrew_anagoria.JPG

23 https://commons.wikimedia.org/wiki/File:Examination_of_a_Witch_-_Tompkins_Matteson.jpg

24 Flominator, CC BY-SA 3.0 <http://creativecommons.org/licenses/by-sa/3.0/>, via Wikimedia Commons: https://commons.wikimedia.org/wiki/File:Fomfr_breast_ripper.jpg

25 https://commons.wikimedia.org/wiki/File:Scoldengravingalpha.jpg

26 https://commons.wikimedia.org/wiki/File:North_Berwick_witches.jpg

27 https://commons.wikimedia.org/wiki/File:North_Berwick_Witches.png

28 https://commons.wikimedia.org/wiki/File:Theresiana-Beinschrauben2.jpg